European Distance and E-Learning Network Annual Conference (EDEN 2020)

Human and Artificial Intelligence for the Society of the Future - Inspiring Digital Education for the Next STE(A)M Student Generation

Timisoara, Romania
22 - 24 June 2020

Editors:

Sandra Kucina Softic
Diana Andone
Andras Szucs

ISBN: 978-1-7138-2384-1

Printed from e-media with permission by:

Curran Associates, Inc.
57 Morehouse Lane
Red Hook, NY 12571

Some format issues inherent in the e-media version may also appear in this print version.

Printed by Curran Associates, Inc. (2021)

European Distance and E-Learning Network (EDEN)
Budapest University of Technology & Economics
H-1111 Budapest, Egry J. u.1.
Hungary

Phone: +36 1 463 1628
Fax: +36 1 463 1858

secretariat@eden-online.org

Additional copies of this publication are available from:

Curran Associates, Inc.
57 Morehouse Lane
Red Hook, NY 12571 USA
Phone: 845-758-0400
Fax: 845-758-2633
Email: curran@proceedings.com
Web: www.proceedings.com

SHORT PAPER BOOK

European Distance and E-Learning Network (EDEN)

Human and Artificial Intelligence for the Society of the Future

Inspiring Digital Education for the Next STE(A)M Student Generation

EDEN 2020 Online Annual Conference

hosted by

Politehnica University of Timisoara, Romania

22-24 June 2020

Edited by

Sandra Kucina Softic, Diana Andone, Andras Szucs
on behalf of the European Distance and E-Learning Network

Introduction

"Education is back where it belongs – at the top of the European policy agenda" stated the European Commission. We intend that Europe will be considered a strong and allied partner to future generations, and that the EU education system must make our societies future proof.

Education is often envisioned in terms of innovation, excellence and competitiveness. But learning is also about reaching personal perfection, using a holistic approach that supports personal and professional development, learner needs and self-realization across different learning environments. Creativity contributes to diversity and innovation, thus Europe's cultural and creative sector is recognized as a substantial resource and driver for innovation and growth.

Digital education has proven to change learning and working practices in the society of today. Intelligence, human and artificial, is in focus, and understanding students and their learning and application of new technologies in education inspires further development.

Skills in Science, Technology, Engineering and Mathematics (STEM) represent an important part of basic literacy in today's knowledge economy. With the inclusion of a critical component – the human being, STE(A)M Education integrates the arts – humanities, languages, dance, drama, music, visual arts, design and digital media. Increasingly, higher education institutions, as well as adult and professional learning are being transformed by intelligent systems that are helping humans learn better and achieve A balanced relation between Artificial and Human intelligence can create trusted, flexible, personalized and inclusive digital learning eco-systems.

For EDEN, the Annual Conference has always been the most important event of the year. It is held every year in June, and our members and partners look forward to it: meeting friends and colleagues, sharing experiences and knowledge, getting new ideas to take with to their workplaces.

In 2020, due to the COVID-19 pandemic, the 29th Annual Conference was held fully online, and albeit completely virtual, We trust that this did not make the conference any less good or interesting than the face to face event.

Because of the pandemic, educators had to adopt new solutions and technologies and to use tools powered by artificial intelligence. The lockdowns and the forced move to online teaching and learning have changed the role of physical space in education and has put pressure on teachers to design new learning environments that are flexible, adaptable, and suitable for a multitude of different users at the same time.

Challenges, brought to all of us by the pandemic, have forced us to move from our safe comfort zones into the unknown. Things we have been talking about for many years have suddenly become necessary and possible and have swiftly pushed teachers, students, and educational institutions into the digital era.

Although the situation has been forced upon us, the pandemic also offers an opportunity to take up the challenge. Let us take advantage of it and jointly find ways for making education and our lives better!

Andras Szucs	Diana Andone	Sandra Kucina Softic
EDEN Secretary General	EDEN Vice President	EDEN President

Acknowledgement and thanks are given to the Programme and Evaluation Committee

Sandra Kucina Softic, EDEN President, University of Zagreb, Croatia

Diana Andone, Politehnica University of Timisoara, Romania

Ulrich Bernath, Ulrich Bernath Foundation for Research in ODL, Germany

Lisa Marie Blaschke, Carl von Ossietzky University of Oldenburg, Germany

Mark Brown, National Institute for Digital Learning, Dublin City University, Ireland

Elena Caldirola, University of Pavia, Italy

Helga Dorner, Central European University, Hungary

Josep Maria Duart, Open University of Catalonia (UOC), Spain

Ulf-Daniel Ehlers, Co-Operative State University Baden-Wurttemberg (DHBW), Germany

Rebecca Galley, The Open University, United Kingdom

Carmen Holotescu, "Ioan Slavici" University Timisoara, Romania

Vlad Mihaescu, Politehnica University of Timisoara, Romania

Mugur Mocofan, Politehnica University of Timisoara, Romania

Don Olcott Jr., Global Higher Education Consultant, Romania

Ebba Ossiannilsson, Swedish Association of Distance Education, Sweden

Wim Van Petegem, Katholieke Universiteit Leuven, Belgium

Antonella Poce, University Roma III, Italy

Timothy Read, National University of Distance Education (UNED), Spain

Alfredo Soeiro, University of Porto, Portugal

Andras Szucs, EDEN, United Kingdom

Ferenc Tatrai, EDEN, United Kingdom

Andrei Ternauciuc, Politehnica University of Timisoara, Romania

Radu Vasiu, Politehnica University of Timisoara, Romania

Silviu Vert, Politehnica University of Timisoara, Romania

TABLE OF CONTENTS

PROJECTS PRESENTED IN THE SYNERGY SESSION

Human and Artificial Intelligence for the Society of the Future
Short Paper Book of the European Distance and E-Learning Network (EDEN)
2020 Annual Conference | Timisoara, 22-24 June, 2020
ISBN 978-615-5511-28-8

EARLY EXPLORATIONS IN ARTIFICIAL INTELLIGENCE (AI) TO RESHAPE LEARNING AND CAPACITY BUILDING

Sheila Jagannathan, The World Bank Group, Open Learning Campus, United States of America

Abstract

The World Bank Group's Open Learning Campus (OLC) is exploring the use of Artificial Intelligence (AI) to reshape and reimagine the learning experience of the future. These include transitioning from long lectures, flat pages of text, one-size-fits-all learning experiences to deeper levels of personalized and adaptive learning. Each learner can have an individualized learning path that recognizes their pre-existing skills and allows the person to move at his or her own pace to achieve the learning outcomes. AI is starting to enable such learning experiences to be personalized at scale. These adaptive programs will be able to monitor how the learner interacts with the system and learns, and analyses the enormous quantities of data generated by a learner's online interactions with ordinary (textbook-like) and extraordinary (game- and social-media-like) content, along with teachers and peers, and with the system itself. Artificial intelligence could offer learners a way to experiment and learn in trial and error method, especially when AI tutors and chatbots can offer solutions for improvement. It not only changes the role of teachers to facilitators but could also improve the curricula and teaching practices.

Introduction

The World Bank Group's Open Learning Campus (OLC) is a free, open source digital and blended learning ecosystem that accelerates development solutions by transforming global knowledge into actionable learning so World Bank (WB) staff, client country governments and the public are exposed to cutting-edge, current and rigorous learning in global development. OLC's existing large and geographically diverse audience base made up of government and non-government officials, in-country policy makers, development practitioners and researchers, and staff from the World Bank Group and other development partners enables and accelerates dissemination of knowledge at a scale. The Open Learning Campus' digital learning environment integrates learning innovations in multimedia, data, gamification, AI and virtual reality offering a unique "mix and match" approach to learning across its three schools:

- WBa Academy – formal, deep dives into development topics in online courses;
- WBx Talks – quick overviews or insights on development and policy-related issues in bite-sized formats;
- WBc Connect – engagement with peer and expert learning and finding crowd-sourced solutions to development challenges.

Personalized and Adaptive Learning

AI Powered, Expert Driven and Collaborative

The Open Learning Campus (OLC) is exploring the use of AI to shape and define the educational experience of the future. These include transitioning from long lectures, flat pages of text, one-size-fits-all learning experiences to deeper levels of personalized and adaptive learning. Each learner can have an individualized learning path that recognizes their pre-existing skills and allows the person to move at his or her own pace to achieve learning outcomes. AI enables such learning to be personalized at scale.

The concept is not entirely new. Learners are interfacing with Artificial Intelligence (AI) when they search in Google, use social media on Facebook and Twitter or buy a book on Amazon. This is all AI-driven and based on recommendations engine. While we may not see humanoid robots acting as teachers within the next decade, there are many initiatives underway that use computer intelligence to help students and teachers get more out of the educational experience. EdTech platforms have started experimenting with personalized learning paths, AI tutors and coaches, eyeball movement tracking and learning analytics to create an experience that suits the learner's skill level, grasping ability, and learning goals.

More broadly, adaptive learning makes content dynamic and interactive, placing the learner at the centre of his or her individual learning experience. The OLC learning ecosystem will be able to monitor how the learner interacts with the system and learns, and analyses the enormous quantities of data generated by a learner's online interactions with ordinary (textbook-like) and extraordinary (game- and social-media-like) content, along with teachers and peers, and with the system itself. The algorithm will have the ability to assess not only what a learner knows now, but also determine what activities and interactions, developed by which providers, delivered in what sequence and medium, increases the possibility of that learner's success.

AI could offer learners a way to experiment and learn in trial and error method, especially when AI tutors and chatbots can offer solutions for improvement. It not only changes the role of teachers to facilitators but could also improves the curriculum and teaching practices. AI helps identify areas where courses (and areas of courses) need to improve. For example, MOOC platforms are putting AI into practice. When many learners are found to submit the wrong answer to a peer assignment, the system alerts the teacher and provides the learner a customized message with hints.

The paper will discuss the use of the following AI tools to increase learner engagement and motivation; reduce dropout rates and enhance teacher effectiveness. The increased effectiveness of AI can be attributed to the improvements in big data analytics and a host of other technologies that have made the collection, curation, modelling, visualization, training and analysis of available data.

Adaptive Learning – Personalized Learning Path

We are currently piloting the Adaptive Learning approach through the course titled, "Regenerating Urban Land: Overview and Global Applications".

Learning objectives:

- Increase city officials' knowledge about good practices and implementation strategies of urban revitalization initiatives by identifying market-viable business models that also maximize the social and economic return of the public sector's investment;
- Review successful case studies and governments' strategies to spur regeneration, including cases focused on development or relocation of government facilities (e.g. Agency HQ) and construction of new parks and/or civic spaces.

For the first time, we have applied an adaptive learning approach that adapts to your existing knowledge, confidence level and schedule. We use sophisticated AI algorithms based on cutting-edge research into how people learn and retain new information. This course analyses and adjusts continuously to what you already know and what you need to study more.

The principle behind the adaptive engine is that it tries to continuously pick the next Learning objective based on a combination of competing needs, which are:

- Driving the student to complete the assignment, resulting in increased knowledge and low dropouts;
- Reinforcing learned material to combat memory decay depletion model, resulting in increased retention;
- Improving the student's self-evaluation to build confidence, resulting in improvement in critical thinking;
- Increasing the confidence of the modelling to reduce the noise in the system, resulting in targeted learning.

Typically, a learning session will start with high-priority questions of medium-difficulty, which are typically answered quickly. Based on the result of the response, the engine will serve up additional questions, exploring the map of the table of contents to assess the overall competency across the curriculum. As the session continues, it will slowly drill down into the most important areas that need the most improvement, increasing the completion and competency in those areas. As the completion rises, the last part of the session will focus on the less important areas, which the student might already know. This modelling focuses on ensuring the most important learning objectives are met. In addition, the engine is mindful of the time taken to solve or complete a certain question, the level of student's engagement, productive persistence and most importantly, her motivation throughout the experience.

Tutor bots – ML Powered Support

AI based tutor bot is an innovative addition to OLC offerings powered by Artificial Intelligence. It will be a tool for learners where they query the bot for frequently asked questions. The bot answers and guides learners to videos and learning resources on questions they have related to the course content. Chatbots are powered by machine learning – which means that the more learners interact with it, the smarter it becomes, and over time with interactions with learners it will get more robust and accurate. The bot will be equipped only to answer questions related to the content and cannot respond to technical issues or questions related to the OLC platform. In that case, the question will be diverted to a human facilitator, who could respond to the question in a timely manner.

Apart from the basic features we are now exploring with voice learning assistants similar to Siri and Alexa. We are also exploring use of bots to nudges and reinforce learning such as reminders on deadlines to complete the course.

The AI bots will support some of the some of the following functions:

- Tips and key points to re-iterate and revise learning on high priority topics;
- Quizzes to quickly assess learner understanding;
- Motivational messages and text reminders to increase course completion rates in MOOCs.

AI Enhanced Video Features – Verified Multilingual Video Subtitles

Language should not be a barrier for learning. Videos with verified subtitles are created easily in 6 languages - English, French, Spanish, Chinese, Russian and Arabic, with the aim to cover the learners from different nonEnglish speaking geographical locations of the Middle East, Asia and Europe regions.

Download Videos and download/print multilingual video transcripts to support learners in low bandwidth environments

Downloading multi-lingual AI-generated transcripts would enable learners to go through videos or podcasts much more quickly, especially in environments with low-internet connectivity with difficulty in streaming or individuals who have difficulty following subtitles. This will overcome the long concentration barrier by providing learners a quick visual aid so they can read the excerpts of the video content comfortably multiple times, thereby allowing in-depth understanding.

Search Video with keyword

Available for English subtitles, the learners can search with specific keyword to spot a section of the video. Once the learner types the word, the result will be displayed with the search keyword highlighted in underline. On clicking on the respective highlighted phrases, the user will be able to view the video from that specific line. This feature is available for online viewing of video. Other language-based search will also be made available as well.

Identify with phrases

For each video or course, based on subtitles a word cloud will be generated. The learner can click the phrases in the word cloud and jump to the respective video narration. The number of times a word appears in the entire video is also given beside each word/phrase. This feature is available for online viewing of videos only.

Jump to sections

Skip to any section using this feature. Typically, speakers jump through different topics and sections throughout the video. Learners can directly jump sections by clicking on the sections listed besides the video. This feature is also available for online viewing of videos only.

Agile Learning – AI Powered Module Development

AI tools are used to create learning modules including supplementary resources in a very short duration, without laborious storyboards and scripts that we are used to. Spaced practice and short answer, and delayed feedback are used to create engaging and interactive module content based on cognitive psychology principles.

Case Study – AI Tutor Bot

The Future of Work: Preparing for Disruption Massive Online Open Course (MOOC)

Executive Summary

The Fourth Industrial Revolution (4IR) in the age of COVID-19 has an unprecedented effect on individuals, institutions, organizations and governments. At a time when the unemployment rate is at a staggering low, one of the most critical subject is the future of work (FOW), the subject of the World Bank Group (WBG) 2019 World Development Report (WDR) and the Future of Work: Preparing for Disruption Massive Online Open Course (MOOC) (https://www.edx.org/course/the-future-of-work-preparing-for-disruption-2)

Alternately, recent advances in technology have disrupted our social and personal lives, overhauling how we live, communicate and do business. Thousands of routine and low-skill jobs will be eliminated by automation, Artificial Intelligence (AI) and digital hyper-connectivity. This course emphasizes the urgency of developing human capital in meeting the challenges of the coming decades. Themes in the course include artificial intelligence, the gig economy, labour market, new technologies, digital economy, machine learning and jobs of the future.

Thirty-four engaging videos by world class experts were the hallmark of the MOOC's success with captions available in six languages (English, Chinese, French, Spanish, Russian and Arabic). Moderated by facilitators, participants engaged in e-discussions to share insightful reflections on course content and to compare country experiences. An Artificial Intelligence (AI) based tutor bot responded to frequently asked questions from learners, with participants overwhelmingly finding the chatbot to be useful.

The MOOC exceeded the WBG's the objective of engaging a large and diverse audience on the future of work, and the related issues of social protection and human capital. The first offering of the course from August 19– September 24, 2019 was highly successful, with over 29,300 participants who signed up for the course, of which 1,128 earned a certificate and 816 earned a certificate of distinction. This led to a second, self-paced offering of the course beginning November 5, 2019 which can be completed over the timespan of a year. We had 31,800 participants in the beginning of Feb 2020 (including facilitated and self-paced) and now we have 40,500 users. In the COVID-19 period from mid of March 2020 to now, there were about 8,000 new enrolments.

Automated Chat FAQs

AI-Powered tutor bot

An Artificial Intelligence (AI) based Tutor Bot, produced exclusively for this course, was employed to deal with Frequently Asked Questions. The chatbot was pre-loaded with technical questions and answers and definitions. Powered by AI, the chatbot could select answers to questions, even if the questions did not perfectly align with the pre-loaded questions.

Summary of Outcomes

Participants overwhelmingly found the chatbot to be useful, although its ability to respond and understand questions could be improved. In the post-course chatbot survey, 80% found the chatbot to be very useful or useful while 10% found the chatbot not to be useful. 32% replied the chatbot had been able to provide the answer to the question they had, 46% found the chatbot was sometimes able to provide the answer to the question they had. 40% found the chatbot understood their question, 40% had a mixed finding, and 6% found it to be painful. 82% found the chatbot intuitive and easy to use, while 8% found it was not intuitive or easy to use.

Human and Artificial Intelligence for the Society of the Future
Short Paper Book of the European Distance and E-Learning Network (EDEN)
2020 Annual Conference | Timisoara, 22-24 June, 2020
ISBN 978-615-5511-28-8

THE ELENE4LIFE DYNAMIC TOOLKIT – A COLLECTION OF ACTIVE LEARNING METHODS FOR SOFT SKILLS DEVELOPMENT TO SUPPORT INNOVATIVE PRACTICE

Magdalena Jasińska, Warsaw University of Technology, Poland, Deborah Arnold, AUNEGe, France

Abstract

The eLene4Life Dynamic Toolkit is a collection of active learning activities and methods, to assist teachers and trainers in implementing innovative approaches to help learners to develop the soft skills required by the labour market, and to play an active role in society. Presented as an open online tool with searchable and downloadable items, the Dynamic Toolkit is grounded in real, innovative practice in both companies and universities.

Short description of the eLene4Life Dynamic Toolkit

The eLene4Life Dynamic Toolkit is designed in order to support the acquisition of soft skills using innovative teaching and training methodologies. It is addressed to educators across Europe, to support them in the process of designing their classes or courses aimed at fostering the development of soft skills by their students.

The eLene4Life Dynamic Toolkit describes a series of innovative practices and related learning activities, taking into consideration the critical issues typical for many universities such as large class sizes (more than 80), rigid physical spaces and the unbalanced relationship between large programmes and limited classroom time.

The teaching and training activities and methods described in the Dynamic Toolkit were collected as part of research conducted in both the education and business sectors in six project partner countries (Belgium, France, Germany, Italy, Poland, UK) within the framework of the eLene4Life Erasmus+ project. For the Higher Education (HE) sector, this involved desk research and interviews with teachers. For the corporate sector, interviews were conducted with the representatives of companies in which innovative training methods are used to help their employees develop soft skills, and with training providers intervening in the field of soft skills for professional and personal development.

In both the HE and corporate sectors, the same data collection scheme was used to enable comparison and analysis, with a view to fostering cross-fertilisation. Out of the 53 methods collected in total, 30 were selected for the Dynamic Toolkit.

To select these, the following main criteria were used for each method/activity:

- Transferability/ease of implementation by teachers;
- Possibility of using it in large groups;
- Assessment of soft skills involved;
- Effectiveness/Positive impact.

Four additional criteria were defined as:

- Engaging learning activities;
- Usage of digital tools;
- Lack of costs;
- Strong research rational.

Characteristics and features of the Dynamic Toolkit

The eLene4Life Dynamic Toolkit is organised as an open online tool with searchable and downloadable items. All collected teaching and learning activities and methods can be filtered using 4 different categories:

- Soft Skills (Digital/Methodological/Personal/social);
- Modes (Blended/Face-to-Face/Online/Outdoor/Other);
- Timings (0-90'/90'-1 day/1 day-1 week/1 week-1 month/1 month-1 semester/Depends on specific scenario);
- Group size (Individual/2-10/11-40/41-80/80+).

After selecting the desired criteria, the list of relevant methods is displayed, and the teacher or trainer can choose the method they are interested in. Each method is described according to the same scheme and contains the following information:

- Description of method;
- Information about: soft skills, group size, mode, duration, tools, costs;
- Scenario of use;
- Assessment;
- Additional resources;
- Connection with other methods.

All this information can be read online or can be download as PDF file for printing if needed. In addition to the description of the methods and activities, a list of digital tools which can be used in active learning is also available as a PDF download. Rather than focusing on the technical mastery of digital tools (which is of course important), these are recommended primarily as support for collaboration, both in learning and at work. Indeed, the aforementioned research showed a significant mismatch between the HE and corporate sectors, with very little recourse to digital tools for soft skills development in HE, compared to a close alignment in the corporate sector where the digital tools used in soft skills training are often those that people actually use in their daily working practices.

To sum up: the eLene4Life Dynamic Toolkit is an easy-to-use, highly-intuitive online tool, collecting the best innovative teaching and training activities and methods to support soft skills development.

Visit the eLene4Life Dynamic Toolkit and try out some of the methods yourself! http://elene4life.eu/dynamic-toolkit/

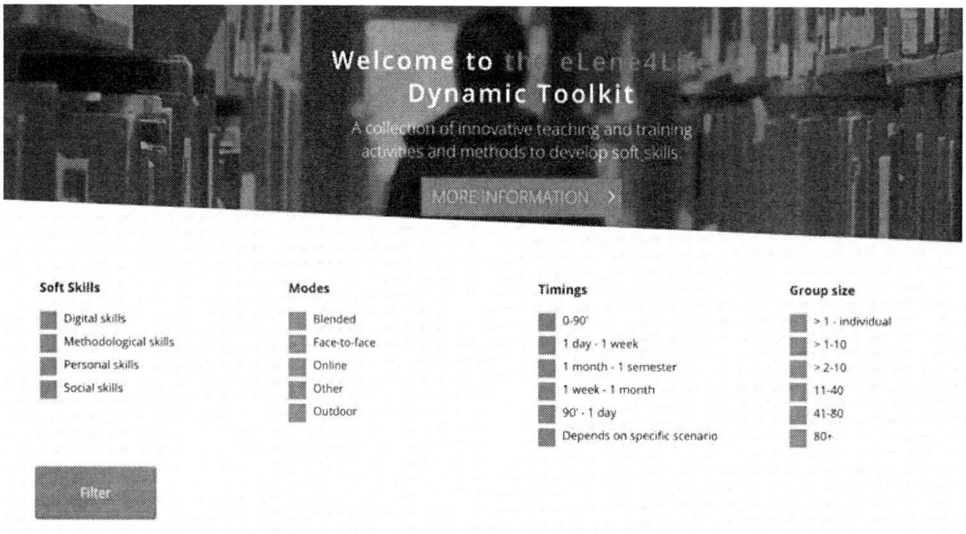

Erasmus+
This project N° 2018-1-FR01-KA203-047829 is funded by the Erasmus+ programme of the European Union.

Human and Artificial Intelligence for the Society of the Future
Short Paper Book of the European Distance and E-Learning Network (EDEN)
2020 Annual Conference | Timisoara, 22-24 June, 2020
ISBN 978-615-5511-28-8

MAINSTREAMING PROCEDURES FOR QUALITY APPRENTICESHIPS IN EDUCATIONAL ORGANIZATIONS AND ENTERPRISES

Naïla Wagner, Svenja Wiechmann, Baden-Wuerttemberg Cooperative State University Heilbronn, Germany

Abstract

In Europe, many young people are affected by unemployment and face challenges in finding quality, stable employment with a decent income (European Union, 2013). An increase of 8.5% was recorded of the youth unemployment rate within 5 years (from 2008 to 2013) (Eurostats, 2013). Internships, apprenticeships and other forms of work-based learning (WBL) are seen as useful devices to give young people access to the labour market and thereby ease the transition between education and future employment (CEDEFOP, 2015; Kuczera, 2017).

However, at present there is no clear EU-wide reference framework or guidance in place for assuring the quality of different types of WBL. It will be key task of the project ApprenticeshipQ to strengthen the cooperation and networking between HVET/PHE institutions and the training site (employers), providing them with innovative practices, future skills development, to establish and enhance quality management procedures that will be developed and tested during the project.

Evidence suggests that WBL can be a promising pathway towards better future employment outcomes for young people. In addition, vocational, technical and professional training combined with work placement can improve future employment, earnings and career outcomes for students. If there is high quality learning in the workplace, young people can be put in situations that help them develop problem-solving abilities and the capacity to adapt to change as they encounter new and different workplace practices, technologies and environments (European Training Foundation, 2013). Assuring quality is key to securing positive outcomes for all stakeholders of the knowledge triangle (HE institutions, world of work and students); and ApprenticeshipQ will therefore focus on approaches to securing and developing high quality apprenticeships/WBL. Particularly focussing on local and regional small and medium enterprises, as the OECD has emphasised, that the quality of local implementation is an important factor that can "make or break" program success (Musset, 2019).

Typology of Quality Apprenticeships

Since there is no common definition for the term apprenticeships, the project consortium has developed the following definition: The process of education, which takes place in shared responsibility between actors from the world of work and education institutions in a learning/education partnership. Apprenticeships can be distinguished into two categories independent and cooperative apprenticeships.

- Independent apprenticeships are organised and managed by employers without any involvement from educational institutions.
- Cooperative apprenticeships are organised and managed in cooperation between educational institutions and employers. These apprenticeships have been distinguished into three subcategories, depending on the governance of an apprenticeship.
- Apprenticeships, where educational institutions and employers share the governance.
- Apprenticeships, with institution led governance.
- Apprenticeships, with employer led governance.

Apprenticeship Quality Criteria and Self-Assessment Online-Tool

Based on the typology of quality apprenticeships and the apprenticeship quality matrix, the consortium conducted a literature review and interviews with employers (n = 30) to identify best practices. This research formed the basis for the development of quality criteria. To validate these criteria, an online survey was designed, and answers from 17 countries were collected. Auditors, quality experts, representatives from HVETs and SMEs, as well as students and alumni were asked to rate these criteria (n = 482). The results indicate that all criteria are perceived as important and should be included in quality management procedures.

The final criteria will be published as an online tool for quality planning by Quality managers in HVET institutions and apprenticeship managers in enterprises.

Quality Apprenticeship Manual for Educational Institutions and Small and Medium Enterprises

To equip HVETS and SMEs with procedures for quality management, the researchers have developed two manuals, describing the quality criteria and their measurement indicators. Furthermore, the manuals contain instruments, methods and tools to implement the quality criteria. This aims at the development of a common quality culture between employers and educational institutions to improve higher vocational education and training.

Outlook

During the final stage of the project, the consortium is going to conduct a piloting with a HVET and a SME to manage and evaluate a set of apprenticeship phases and therefore implement the quality management. Interviews with national experts of apprenticeship quality management will be held to develop harmonisation guides as well as policy recommendations. During workshops, as participant and presenter at international conferences, the results are going to be validated.

References

CEDEFOP. (2015). High-performance apprenticeships & work-based learning: 20 guiding principles. Retrieved from http://www.cedefop.europa.eu/hr/toolkits/vet-toolkit-tackling-early-leaving/resources/highperformanceapprenticeships-work-based

European Training Foundation. (2013). Work-based learning: Benefits and Obstacles. A literature review for policy makers and social partners in EFT partner countries. Retrieved from https://www.etf.europa.eu/en/publicationsand-resources/publications/work-based-learning-benefits-and-obstacles-literature

European Union (2013). Apprenticeship and Traineeship Schemes in EU27: Key Success Factors – A guidebook for Policy Planners and Practitioners. Retrieved from https://ec.europa.eu/social/main.jsp?catId=1045

Eurostat. (2013). March 2013 - Euro Area Unemployment Rate at 12.1%, Eurostat News Release, 30.4.2013. Retrieved from http://epp.eurostat.ec.europa.eu/cache/ITY_PUBLIC/3-30042013-BP/EN/3-30042013-BPEN.PDF

Kuczera, M. (2017). Striking the right balance: Costs and benefits of apprenticeship. *OECD Education Working Papers, No. 153.* Paris: OECD Publishing.

Musset, P. (2019). Improving Work-based learning in schools. *OECD Social, Employment and Migration Working Papers No. 233.* Retrieved from http://www.oecd.org/officialdocuments/publicdisplaydocumentpdf/?cote=DELSA/ELSA/WD/SEM(2019)12&docLa nguage=En

Human and Artificial Intelligence for the Society of the Future
Short Paper Book of the European Distance and E-Learning Network (EDEN)
2020 Annual Conference | Timisoara, 22-24 June, 2020
ISBN 978-615-5511-28-8

LOS ANGELES TO NOVOSIBIRSK, FROM KIRUNA TO CAPE TOWN – EARLY EXPERIENCES WITH THE BAVARIAN VIRTUAL UNIVERSITY'S NEW OPEN ONLINE COURSE PROGRAM: OPEN VHB

Alexander von Stetten, Steffi Widera, Virtuelle Hochschule Bayern (vhb) / Bavarian Virtual University, Germany

Abstract

For 20 years, the Bavarian Virtual University (Ger.: Virtuelle Hochschule Bayern, abbr.: vhb), an association of 31 universities in Bavaria (Germany), has been offering curriculum-based, complete online courses for the students of its member universities. But in July 2019, the vhb broke new ground and expanded its range to include open online courses for everyone. The launch of the new open online course program OPEN vhb has been very positive. As of 31.01.2020, 39 courses were available and around 20,000 learners had already registered on the new platform. Another 35 courses were under development at the same time. In the open online courses, which can be used by anyone free of charge, university knowledge becomes freely accessible. The courses are developed and offered by professors of the vhb's member universities. In the courses, particular importance is attached to an interactive and media-didactically appealing design of the learning content.

Introduction

When the Bavarian Virtual University (Ger.: Virtuelle Hochschule Bayern, abbr.: vhb) announced its plans in 2018 to soon launch a new open online course program in addition to its existing learning offerings, some people thought: Another MOOC platform? Who needs it? Who should take the courses? Such questions seem quite justified given the large number of MOOC platforms around the world. However, compared to other MOOC providers, the vhb's new open online course program OPEN vhb is characterized by some special features, to which we will refer to below. These might have contributed to the successful start of the platform. Indeed, the start was definitely successful. Since the opening of OPEN vhb in July 2019, within a short time people eager to learn from everywhere, from Los Angeles to Novosibirsk, from Kiruna to Cape Town, have enrolled in the new online courses. From zero to 18,000 participants in only five months, without spending any money on commercial advertising, clearly shows that OPEN vhb has hit the nerve of time. There is a demand for open university courses as well as a desire to learn for a lifetime.

OPEN vhb: The vhb's New Open Online Course Program

Background

First, we would like to take a brief look at where the vhb comes from, what it actually is and what it has offered as of yet. Founded in 2000, the vhb is an association of 31 universities in Bavaria (Germany), 27 of which are state universities and 4 of which are state-accredited universities under church sponsorship. The vhb is primarily funded by the Bavarian State Ministry for Science and Art. So far the vhb has focused its activities on one specific offer named CLASSIC vhb. In its CLASSIC vhb course program, the vhb has been providing online courses for students of its member universities for 20 years. Following the vhb's basic principle of cooperation between universities, a CLASSIC vhb course is always anchored in the curricula of at least two member universities. CLASSIC vhb courses are primarily aimed at students of the vhb's member universities. Only these students can use CLASSIC vhb courses free of charge and thus supplement their on-campus studies with online courses at any time and place. In every CLASSIC vhb course, a graded final examination is offered and credit points (ECTS) can be acquired. The courses are tied to the universities' semester calendar. In the summer semester 2020 the CLASSIC vhb course program comprises more than 550 curricular online courses from 15 subject groups, which are attended by more than 30,000 students from the vhb's member universities.

Having previously merely focused on the CLASSIC vhb course program, the vhb broke new ground during the past year. Parallel to the CLASSIC vhb course program, a new open online course program is available for all interested parties since July 2019: OPEN vhb

Motivation for the Introduction of OPEN vhb

The new initiative OPEN vhb is part of the state master plan for Bavaria's digital future. The motivation for the introduction of OPEN vhb was to fulfil the universities' social educational mission to offer further scientific education in the sense of lifelong learning to an interested general public. In doing so, target groups relevant to the universities (e.g., school graduates, prospective students, students from abroad) should also be tapped. Furthermore, OPEN vhb should offer universities, faculties, chairs and last but not least professors an opportunity to present themselves and their topics, fields of work, and research priorities. This should also help to highlight the attractiveness of Bavaria as a university location and further increase its visibility and range in this respect.

Features and Criteria of OPEN vhb

"What is right, what is wrong? Is that really true? Where can I find reliable answers, assured knowledge?" In short: How can you further educate yourself in a simple and easy way? The open online course program OPEN vhb is designed to help those with a thirst for knowledge to find answers to these and many other questions and thus support them in broadening their personal horizons.

With the courses (https://open.vhb.org) the Bavarian universities open up to the general public and make university knowledge freely accessible. They are complete online courses developed and offered by professors of Bavarian universities. The courses can be attended by anyone free of charge – you neither need to be enrolled at university nor do you need a university entrance qualification. In the courses, university knowledge is prepared and imparted in a comprehensible form and free of any curricular requirements. In doing so, particular emphasis is placed on innovative media-didactics and an interactive way of knowledge transfer. The OPEN vhb course program does not focus on a limited range of topics but serves a wide variety of knowledge areas. At present, the program includes, for example, language courses (e.g., "Smarter German. German as a second foreign language – after English", course language: English), courses focusing on economic topics (e.g., "Leadership in the Digital Age", English), medical courses (e.g., "Orthopedics – Behind the Scenes", German) or courses dealing with classical key qualifications (e.g., "Key Competence Spelling", German) and other important everyday topics (e.g., "In Search of a Sustainable Development", German).

Registration on the OPEN vhb platform only requires a few clicks and can be done via web form or with your Facebook or Google account. After registration, you can enrol in every currently running course and start work on the course content on your own (i.e., in self-study). Each course is offered continuously for a minimum period of five years. You can join an ongoing course at any time; for example, the courses are not tied to the universities' semester calendar and therefore do not pause during the semester break. In most courses, you have the opportunity to download an ungraded certificate of participation after course completion. As soon as you have passed the online self-tests required in the respective course, the download is available. In some courses, you can also receive badges. In OPEN vhb courses, no graded exams are offered and no credit points (ECTS) can be earned. In contrast to several other MOOC providers, OPEN vhb does not offer an additional service where you can get a graded certificate for a fee. Furthermore, OPEN vhb courses are quality assured, not only because they are developed and offered by university professors but also because each course is evaluated by external experts immediately after its start and every two and a half years thereafter.

The similarities and differences between CLASSIC and OPEN vhb courses are again summarized in Figure 1.

CLASSIC vhb (courses)		OPEN vhb (courses)
• Complete online courses	=	• Complete online courses
• Developed by professors from Bavarian universities	=	• Developed by professors from Bavarian universities
• Quality assured	=	• Quality assured
• Target group: students	≠	• Target group: all interested parties
• Free of charge only for students of the vhb's member universities	≠	• Free of charge for everybody
• Curricularly anchored	≠	• Free of any curricular requirements
• Tutorial support	≠	• Self learning environments
• Graded examination, graded certificate, Credit Points (ECTS)	≠	• No graded examination, ungraded certificate of participation, no Credit points (ECTS)
• Tied to the universities' semester calendar	≠	• Continuously available for at least 5 years

Figure 1. CLASSIC and OPEN vhb courses in comparison

Learning Platform

At its core, the learning platform on which the OPEN vhb courses are offered is a Moodle system, which has been significantly modified and adapted to the challenges of open online courses.

First of all, OPEN vhb courses do not make use of a Moodle core course format like the *week* or the *topic* format. Instead, the courses are presented in a specially developed course format, which is based on chapters and lessons (cf., Figure 2). Each chapter consists of several lessons, which contain the actual learning content. Embedding plays a major role in the presentation of the learning content. For example, videos and tests/quizzes are embedded and displayed directly in the lessons, just like text or pictures. The goal is that learners no longer have to open separate files and leave the course structure to be able to access certain contents. Instead, they should ideally be able to see the whole learning content of a course and work on it directly on the lesson pages.

Furthermore, the OPEN vhb course format contains a central menu bar. Here, learners can find a news forum, a discussion board, the list of participants, social media channels related to the course, and an area where they can download open badges and/or the certificate of participation as soon as they have passed the required tests.

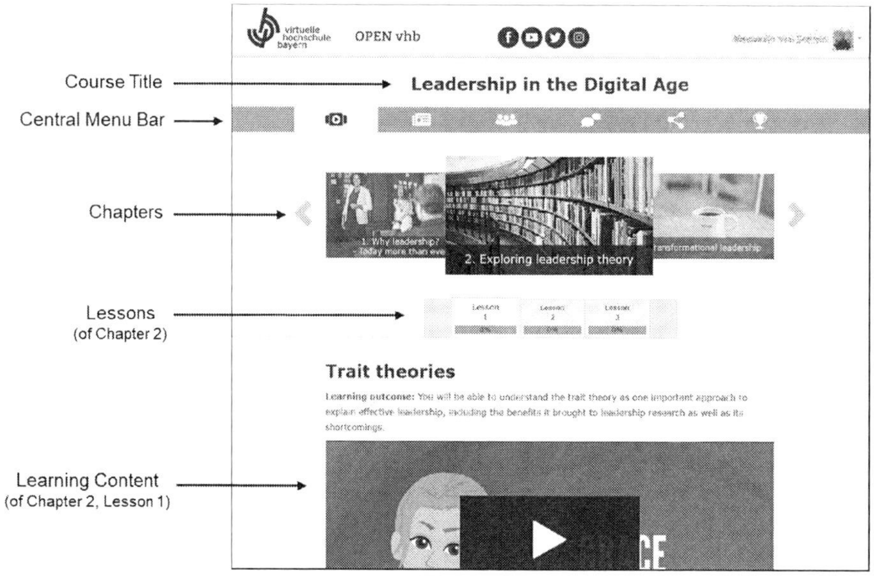

Figure 2. The OPEN vhb course format

Because OPEN vhb courses aim at a varied and interactive presentation of the learning content, the tool H5P (https://h5p.org) is of particular importance. H5P is integrated into the platform via a plug-in and offers numerous different content types that can be used to develop and present learning content in an interactive way. However, other proven external tools and services, such as LearningApps.org, Learning Snacks or Padlet, can also be used in the courses to enable intuitive and varied learning with different media (text, image, video, audio, quizzes etc.).

Potentials for Data Analysis

With regard to the vhb's motivation for the introduction of OPEN vhb and its future development, it would be desirable and, of course, beneficial to know the actual course participants better. Have the initially defined target groups been reached? Are there other user groups that were not considered in advance? What motivates people to use the open courses? How old are the course participants? Are the open courses used in companies for further training purposes? Do individuals use the courses to increase their personal career opportunities? Are courses used in the transition between school and university? If so, do participants tend to study afterwards or not?

All these parameters are not yet queried. The entry threshold to access the courses is deliberately kept low. In accordance with the European data protection regulation as little personal data as necessary is collected. However, it would be desirable to have access to more data to be able to tailor OPEN vhb even better to the target groups in future. Therefore, the collection of such data on a voluntary basis is currently being discussed.

Conclusion: The Importance of Openness

Universities, including those in Germany, are becoming increasingly transparent and are opening their lecture halls in virtual space. In the spirit of this openness, the social mission beyond the education of young people in a classic way is being taken more and more seriously. For in times in which there is often talk of a widening gap between educated and educationally deprived classes, the importance of open educational formats is steadily increasing.

On the other hand, open online courses also help universities to sharpen their profile. Only with their websites or with their appearances in social media universities are quickly reaching their limits when trying to present their specific advantages in a truly transparent and understandable way. But taking a closer look at the way teaching actually takes place makes a university – even in virtual space – tangible and accessible.

Human and Artificial Intelligence for the Society of the Future
Short Paper Book of the European Distance and E-Learning Network (EDEN)
2020 Annual Conference | Timisoara, 22-24 June, 2020
ISBN 978-615-5511-28-8

USE OF IMMERSIVE REALITY TO TRAIN CONSTRUCTION SAFETY

Alfredo Soeiro, Joao Pocas Martins, University of Porto, Portugal, Nicholaos Theodossiou, Aristotle University of Technology, Greece, Ivica Zavrski, University of Zagreb, Croatia, Peter Mesaros, University of Kosice, Slovakia

Abstract

Construction sites are dynamic and complex environments, making them difficult to control and monitor. Construction safety prevents people from dying or becoming incapacitated. It is a socially relevant issue that persists despite several initiatives. To cope with the pressure of avoiding accidents development, safety can no longer rely on traditional accident preventions measures. The project is co-funded by the Erasmus+ Programme of the European Union and arises from the synergy between higher education institutions and construction company provider to implement the use of smart technologies in proper training. The digital tools allow the creation of instruments that simulate construction scenarios allowing the identification and prevention of risks for teachers, technicians, and engineers. This approved project aims at enhancing knowledge exchange between representatives of three sectors to innovate the accident prevention approaches through effective collaboration between researchers in the virtual reality filed and construction companies. The project will develop innovative and interactive IR (Immersive Reality) solutions based on BIM modelling capacities to prevent accidents and train workers. The project intends to create usable tools for teachers, technicians, and engineers that will be used in any construction project. Project also aims at offering training sessions online on an online platform (project website, wiki) to grant learners and trainees access to interactive material and resources. These tools range from applications to be used on smartphones to virtual reality contexts depending on the needs of training.

Novel Characteristics: Training with Immersive Reality and Simulation

Project design was based on joint analysis and on partners' know-how and experience, to propose viable solutions. The specific aims for the projected are:

- Developing, implementing, validating and tuning of interactive IR approaches to promote multidiscipline creativity, innovative thinking, and practical skills in the digital era;

- Ensuring education and research are mutually reinforcing, and strengthening the role of institutions in their local and regional environments;
- Explore synergies and stimulate greater dialogue between HE, enterprises and VET schools, in the scope of community and outreach activities;
- Supporting the civic and social responsibility of students, workers, engineers and technicians.

To elaborate on the previously mentioned aims and objectives the project includes:

- Contribute indirectly to encourage VET and HEI students and staff to get involved in construction safety;
- Project intends to promote best practice exchanges, supporting the development of more varied teaching methods and personalized training, in accordance with the 2012 "Bucharest Communication" (Ministerial Conference-EHEA) recommendation of promoting "student-centred learning" characterised by innovative methods of teaching;
- Project pedagogic development, together with its activities, are expected to mobilise institutions, teachers, engineers, workers and technicians. The project interactive learning tools development and maintenance of an open, collaborative repository, tutorials and operational guides that support the performance of specific tasks;
- Contribute towards the development and application of tools and practical guides for architects and engineers involved in construction design.

By taking into consideration the listed aims the project will be achieving and focusing on the collaboration and knowledge exchange between the HEI/VET organizations and construction companies. In addition, the advancement and innovation in a human resources education and training perspective may benefit the construction companies and helping the development of an entrepreneurial mind set and foster future cooperation. Nevertheless, allowing the collaboration between HE and enterprises the project may develop the creation of an educational and training strategy that may boost the health and safety competences and investment in construction industries.

Features to be demonstrated – Effectiveness of training and validation of competences

The project is following a collaborative and hands-on strategy to learning, integrating a broad vision concerning a project where the activities establish a very close and interconnected cooperation, where the exchange of co-creation of knowledge between HEIs and construction companies is a key factor. This methodology defines the responsibilities of the stakeholders during the project and within all its phases. Furthermore, the tools to support an enhanced cooperation are defined as well as the training sessions to convey the competences (knowledge, skills and attitudes) necessary to prevent accidents in construction.

Therefore, the project's activities will encompass different types of international activities that will happen in the partner countries to fulfil the project vision. These will require the development of equipment and of software resources (innovative use of integrated IR tools), online content and digital platforms (supporting the dissemination of knowledge, the training and the validation of results), and collaborative processes (to facilitate group and exchange cooperation). This intends to portrait the work reality of collaborative teams needed to prevent accidents in construction sites. The project development of realistic simulations based on existing developments and respective adaptations will provide to all those involved the possibility of experiencing a practical learning and training approach in a virtual environment like the one they may find in their future construction sites.

The tasks were developed according to the expertise of each partner. Besides project management, and quality assurance tasks, the project activities were divided into 4 main groups. Preparation with identification of the state of art in the field strategies, solution, trainings, studies, technologies etc. and selection of an online platform for interaction with users and content developers. Development and implementation address the physical content of interactive IR tools and learning content with development of interactive simulations, IR models and simulations, written materials/manuals, and other forms of pedagogical publications. Validation and tuning are dedicated to development of activities in laboratories, construction sites, workshops and other facilities and testing of the learning tools amongst other HEIs so they can be improved, gauged and validated. The exploitation and dissemination events will consider user participation and location, activities can be divided in three main groups (lab centred events, site centred activities, online activities) and content will be developed to allow use in different environments.

References

Antwi-Afari, M. F., Li, H., Pärn, E. A., & Edwards, D. J. (2018). Critical success factors for implementing building information modelling (BIM): A longitudinal review. *Automation in Construction, 91*, 100–110. https://doi.org/10.1016/j.autcon.2018.03.010

Getulia, V., Caponea, P., Bruttinia, A., & Isaac, S. (2020). BIM-based immersive Virtual Reality for construction workspace planning: A safety-oriented approach. *Automation in Construction, 114*. https://doi.org/10.1016/j.autcon.2020.103160

Nnaji, C., & Karakhan, A. (2020). Technologies for safety and health management in construction: Current use, implementation benefits and limitations, and adoption barriers. *Journal of Building Engineering, 29*. https://doi.org/10.1016/j.jobe.2020.101212

Human and Artificial Intelligence for the Society of the Future
Short Paper Book of the European Distance and E-Learning Network (EDEN)
2020 Annual Conference | Timisoara, 22-24 June, 2020
ISBN 978-615-5511-28-8

STOP MRSA– A VIRTUAL REALITY GAME PROMOTING A CLINICAL GUIDELINE TO PREVENT MRSA INFECTION

Grete Oline Hole, Faculty of Health and Social Sciences, Atle B. Geitung, Daniel Patel, Harald Soleim, Oskar Bråten, Trygve E. Igesund, Faculty of Engineering, Western Norway University of Applied Sciences, Eva C. Backer, ICT-dept, Western Norway Health Authority, Norway

Abstract

This paper presents the development of a virtual reality game-based education tool for Norwegian health personnel. The education tool introduces a stepwise presentation of the evidence-based clinical guidelines to prevent and reduce Methicillin-resistant Staphylococcus aureus (MRSA) in a hospital setting. Through the Virtual Reality user experience and interact with computer generated simulations of the hospital admission of a patient with a potential MRSA-infection. The game was developed in a productive collaboration between the Western Norway Health Authority, Haukeland University hospital and the Department of Computer Science, Electrical Engineering and Mathematical Sciences and the Department of Health and Social Sciences at Western Norway University of Applied Sciences.

Introduction

Infections have for thousands of years represented a global challenge for health. With the exploration of medicines as penicillin late in the 1940ties, great expectations towards a drug-based solution against infections were raised. Unfortunately, it quickly became clear that bacteria and germs rapidly adapt strategies against antibiotic treatment. There now exist bacteria which have developed resistance against all existing antibiotics. The most common of these is the Methicillin-resistant Staphylococcus Aureus (MRSA) (MRSA-veilederen, 2009).

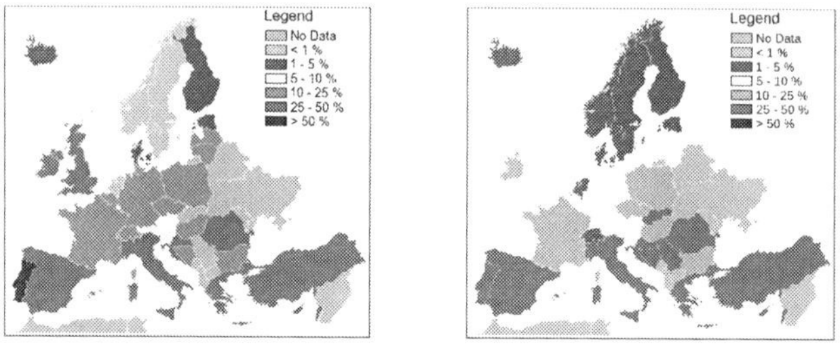

Figure 1. Incidence of MRSA in human blood sample. Left: year 2008. Right: year 2017 (RIVM XXX)

As shown in Figure 1, Norway, along with other Nordic countries, have had few occurrences of MRSA. However, recent studies show that its prevalence has increased over the last decade, although it is still low compared to the rest of the world (Ruscio et al., 2017).

The solution towards the MRSA threat is to keep a strict hygienic schedule to inhibit and control potential infections. For this, there have been developed guidelines for medical- and healthcare organisations which specify the exact steps a practitioner should follow in order to detect and handle such infections (WHO, 2009). The outbreak of COVID-19, and the resulting restrictions imposed by the government all over the world, has further emphasised the need for health personnel awareness of such hygienic procedures.

This paper presents a game-based digital educational tool for healthcare practitioners made in Virtual Reality. The tool represents gamification of the steps in the local regional health authority, Helse Bergen's MRSA-infection clinical practice control guideline (MRSA veilederen, 2009), and is designed to train students and new employees within health care in Norway on MRSA mitigation. By gamifying the guideline, one goal is that training becomes more engaging and that also skilled personnel will try the tool. The game was made in VR to create a more realistic training environment. Another goal is to raise awareness of the serious problem of MRSA-infections in an entertaining way.

Background

Within the medical and health domain it is crucial to be updated and trained on the latest diagnostic procedures, treatment and care. Earlier knowledge and skills can become outdated and do damage instead of cure, and in an area of rapid clinical advances and an information explosion, evidence from valid research with clinical expertise and patient values within the actual setting must be combined (Sackett et al., 1996). This leads to a constant focus on life-long learning with continuous professional development, innovation and interprofessional collaboration. In accordance, the last years have shown an increasing motivation for avoiding unwanted variations and unwanted events through the "vision of zero incidents". (IOM, 2000). A tool towards this goal is the development and implementation of clinical practice guidelines.

Clinical Practice Guidelines (CPG)

A clinical practice guideline is a set of systematically developed statements to assist practitioners and patients' decisions about the appropriate health care for a specific circumstance. A well-developed guideline promotes best practice, reducing unwanted variations in care, improves diagnostic accuracy and promotes the best therapies. (Grimshaw et al., 2012; NCBI, 2016; Shekelle, 2020). Unfortunately, there is gap between recommended treatment and care from the evidence presented in the guideline, and clinical practice (IOM, 2001; Nyameino et al., 2019). Therefore, efforts are taken to promote the uptake of CPG's by making them easily accessible for health personnel (Shiffman, Michel, Essaihi, & Thornquist, 2004; Goud et al., 2009; Nyameino et al., 2019).

Teaching and learning within health services

There is a distinction between formal postgraduate education, such as a master's degree in clinical nursing offered and credited by a university, and the continuous professional training within a workplace or the employer's training facilities. The latter can be traditional staff development based on workshops and short-courses, or a more random training as a quality improvement initiative. According to the best practices of teaching adults (Taylor & Hamdy, 2013), staff should be able to assess the actual learning material when they experience a need for this knowledge and/or skill, Just In Time-learning (Riel, 2002).

Simulation / Scenario-based learning

Simulation is widely used in healthcare as a way of facilitating training within a safe environment. It is an educational tool where the learner physically interacts to mimic an aspect of clinical care for the purpose of teaching or assessment (Brygdes et al., 2015; Mikkelsen, Reime, & Harris, 2008). Learners interact with people, simulators, computers or task trainers to accomplish learning goals that are representative of the learner's real-world responsibilities (Lioce, 2020). The simulated environment often resembles the workplace (Lamb, Annetta, Firestone, & Etiopio, 2018).

Education Technology (EdTech) for health professions

Traditional didactic teaching has shown to have the lowest retention rate regarding knowledge and skill, while a more dynamic educational environment may enhance retention and reinforce learning (Reed et al., 2014). Research confirms that the accelerated feedback to the learner enabled by technology promotes effective learning (McGaghie, Issenberg, Petruse, & Scalese, 2016). Further on, several studies show a significant overall effect of web-based education for delivering basic knowledge and clinical performance for all health professional. (Abdulmajed, Park, & Tekian, 2015; Cook et al., 2011; Kang & Seomun, 2018).

Technology enhanced simulation

Following Kirkpatrick's model for evaluation of learning outcomes within medical training (Kirkpatrick & Kirkpatrick, 2006), technology-enhanced simulation training in health professions education has shown to be associated with large positive effects for outcomes of knowledge, skills and behaviour and moderate effects for patient-related outcomes. (Cook et al., 2012; Cook, Erwin, & Triola, 2010). However, such training is a complex service intervention that needs to be planned and practiced with attention to organisational contexts. Successful simulation by technology requires carefully selected and sequenced instructional events for the simulated task, appropriate faculty development, and institutional commitment (Cook et al., 2011; McGaghie et al., 2016).

Gamification

Gamification as an instruction method to promote learning can make a positive impact on the achieved skills and knowledge. (Abdulmajed et al., 2015; Akl et al., 2010; Subash & Cudney, 2018). Here one applies game design to a variety of processes with the goal of increasing player motivation, which in turn can help to enhance engagement and time spent playing.

Virtual Reality (VR)

Reality technology has improved recent years, in part thanks to advances in tracking, display technology and computational power. VR applications can be divided into three main categories: Games, where the goal is for the player to have fun; simulators that closely mimics real-world scenarios; and non-interactive experiences, where the player mainly acts as an observer, as if on a visit to a museum. A gamified application will fall somewhere between the first two categories. Simulation and gaming have proven to be useful to teach CPG. (Cook, Erwin, & Trimola, 2010; Goud et al., 2009; Nyameino et al., 2019). By combing these with VR, the user can experience and interact with computer generated simulations in a highly immersive manner. It primarily does so by reducing external visual stimulation and providing alternative visual stimuli with a head-mounted display. Immersion can be increased further by providing other types of sensory stimuli, such as auditory and haptic.

The VR Game: "Stop MRSA"

In the VR training game called "Stop MRSA", the playthrough is designed to cover all the steps in the CPG for MRSA made at Haukeland University Hospital. As we can see in Figure 2, the first task is to select a patient that needs to be screened based on the screening criteria. For training, the player is presented with four patients with accompanying medical information. One of the four patients fulfil the requirements for MRSA screening according to the guidelines. The player needs to identify this patient and perform correct following steps. The user is scored based on the decisions that are made.

Figure 2 shows the admission steps of the CPG from Haukeland University Hospital. Building upon both international as well as national recommendations, the same procedure will take place all over Norway.

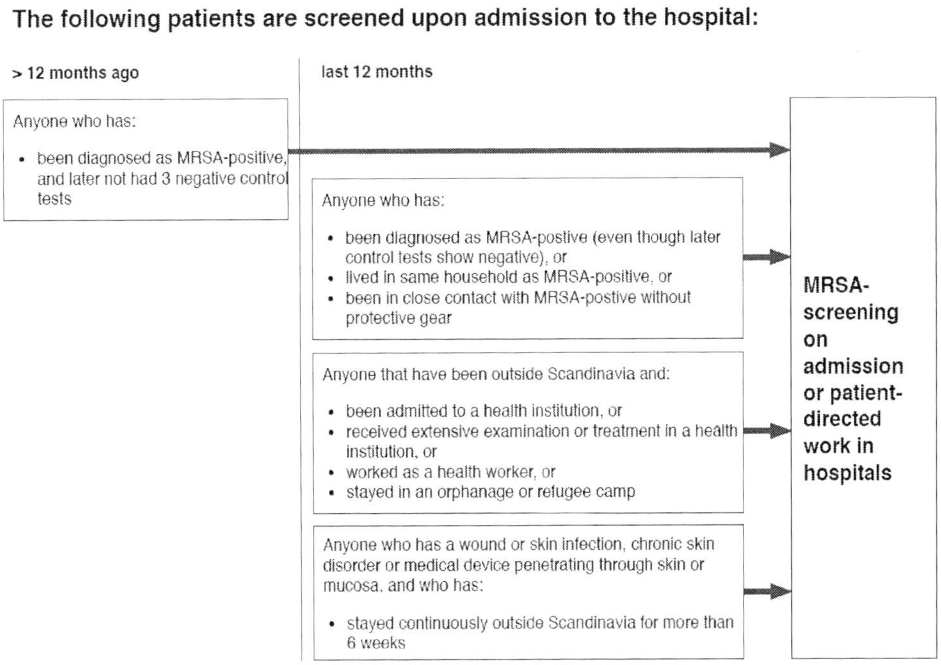

Figure 2. MRSA guideline for Haukeland University Hospital

The locations where MRSA-samples are to be taken are: both nostrils (same swab); throat including tonsils; perineum (the space between the anus and scrotum or vulva); wounds; eczema; puss; scars from infection or active skin diseases; around insertion site for foreign matter (catheter, drainage, tracheostomy, etc.) and catheter urine.

The playthrough is designed to cover all the steps in the guideline. Figure 3 shows the flow diagram of the game which reflects the MRSA guideline. The flow goes from left to right when correct actions are performed.

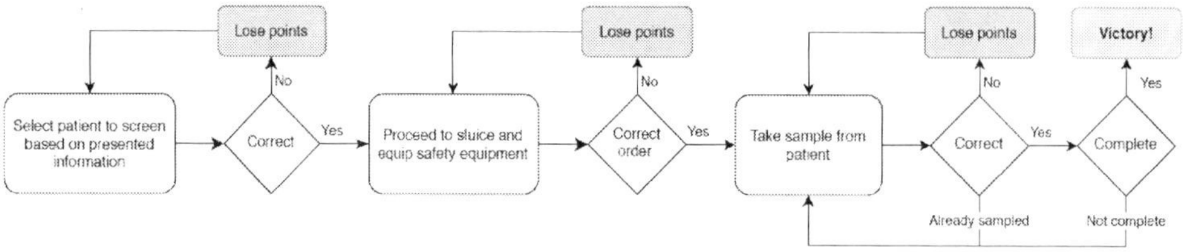

Figure 3. Flow diagram of game.

Technology

The game was made using the Unity game engine (2020). To make the VR user-interface, Unity's XR interaction toolkit (2020) is used. There exist other VR toolkits such as Oculus Integration (2020) and SteamVR (2020). However, Oculus Integration is limited to Oculus Head Mounted Display (HMD)s, while SteamVR is limited to computer powered HMDs and will not support stand-alone HMDs such as the Oculus Quest. Because we wanted the game to be available and supported on as many HMDs as possible, including stand-alone HMDs, we found the XR interaction toolkit to work well. We extensively tested our solution on the Oculus Quest HMD and the HTC Vive Pro HMD.

The Oculus Quest HMD is a stand-alone HMD which does not require a wired connection to a computer, it therefore felt natural to wear due to the lack of wirings and would be practical to transport to testing/training sites. Since the computer is embedded in the HMD, it does not handle large graphics scenes. Therefore, we had to spend some time on the graphics in the game, so that it was lightweight and would run smoothly on the HMD.

Results

The playthrough is designed to cover all the steps in the MRSA guideline. As we can see in Figure 3, the first task is to select a patient that needs to be screened based on the screening criteria.

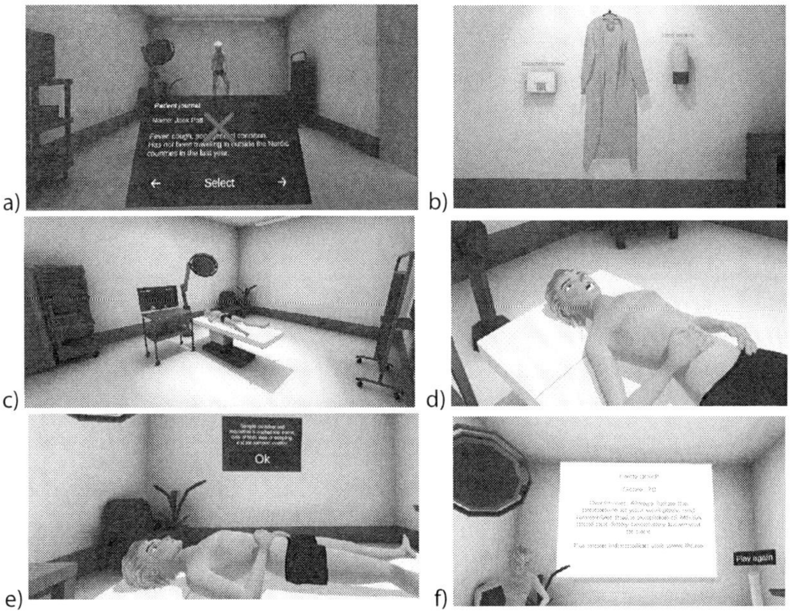

Figure 4. Selected scenes from the gameplay. a) Browsing through patient information and selection of which patient to screen. Here is indicated with a cross that a wrong patient was selected for screening. b) selection of safety equipment to use, order must be correct also. c) MRSA sampling room with different equipment that can be used for sampling. d) Sampling patient's throat with swab. e) Educational information is displayed during gameplay. f) A synopsis of the results is shown at the end of the game.

The player is presented with four patients, shown on the other side of a window, and can read their medical information, see Figure 4a). One of the four patients should be screened for MRSA. Choosing the wrong patient will give result in a loss of points, but the player can keep trying until the correct patient is chosen. When a correct patient is chosen, a sluice must be entered before taking the samples, see Figure 4b). In the sluice, a prompt will appear that informs the player that they should wash their hands before putting on the safety equipment. Once the player has done this, the last door will open leading the player to the room where the patient is located, see Figure 4c). Beside the bed there is a table with tools you can grab. Some of the tools one must use, while others are not relevant and will only lead to a loss of points if applied. The patient has a set of loci on their body that must be screened. The throat (Figure 4d), perineum and nostrils are places which are required for all patients, and some also have a wound and/or urinary catheter that needs to be sampled. Each successful sampling attempt is rewarded with points and the name of the locus is added to a visible list such that the player can track its progress. Unsuccessful screening attempts will remove the tool from your hand, take away some of your points and make a "negative" sound effect. Once the last location is successfully screened, a prompt appears. It informs the player how samples should be marked before they are dispatched for testing (Figure 4e). At the end, a screen rolls down, presenting the player with their score, a rough assessment of how they did, and a disclaimer that they should follow the guidelines of their own hospital (Figure 4e). In addition to this, text will appear on the wall with a summary of the guideline, specifically who should be screened and where on the body they should be screened. The purpose of this is to make sure the player understands why what they did was correct or incorrect. The user can press a "Play again" button for the players who wish to play through the game again with a new set of patients.

Conclusions

Throughout the development process of the software, numerous challenges arose surrounding areas such as cross-platform compatibility, identifying and implementing gamified aspects of the guideline, user interaction design and performance optimization. These issues were solved in close collaboration with the staff from Helse-Bergen who initiated this gamification of the MRSA guideline. The plan was to perform thoroughly evaluations of the game on large groups but due to the Corona pandemic, this was not possible. Feedback from both the development-process as well as the few who evaluated the final version, revealed that the game may be a useful tool for teaching and reminding medical personnel how to handle MRSA. However, more importantly might that it is a proof-of concept implementation meant to create attention on MRSA in an engaging and interesting way.

References

Akl, E. A., Pretorius, R. W., Sackett, K., Erdley, W. S., Bhoopathi, P. S., Alfarah, S., & Schünemann, H. J. (2010). The effect of educational games on medical students' learning outcomes: A systematic review: BEME Guide No 14. *Medical Teacher, 32*(1), 16-27. doi: 10.3109/01421590903473969

Abdulmajed, H., Park, Y. S., & Tekian, A. (2015). Assessment of educational games for health professions: A systematic review of trends and outcomes. *Medical Teacher, 37*, S25-S32.

Brydges, R., Hatala, R, Zendejas, B, Erwin, P. J., & Cook, D. A. (2015). Linking simulation-based educational assessments and patient-related outcomes: a systematic review and metaanalysis. *Acad Med., 90*(2), 246-56.

Cook, D. A., Erwin, P. J., & Triola, M. M. (2010). Computerized Virtual Patients in Health Professions Education: A Systematic Review and Meta-Analysis. *Acad Med., 85*, 1589–1602.

Cook, D. A., Hatala ,R., Brydges, R., Zendejas, B., Szostek, J. H., Wang, A. T., Erwin, P. J., & Hamstra, S. J. (2011). Technology-enhanced simulation for health professions education: a systematic review and meta-analysis. *Journal American Medical Association, 306*(9), 978-88.

Cook, D. A., Brydges, R., Hamstra, S. J., Zendejas, B., Szostek, J. H., Wang, A. T., Erwin, P. J., & Hatala, R. (2012). Comparative effectiveness of technology-enhanced simulation versus other instructional methods: a systematic review and meta-analysis. *Simul Healthc., 7*(5), 308-20.

Goud, R., de Keizer, N. F., ter Riet, G., Wyatt, J. C., Hasman, A., Hellemans, I. M., & Peek, N. (2009). Effect of guideline based computerised decision support on decision making of multidisciplinary teams: cluster randomised trial in cardiac rehabilitation. *Bmj, 338*, b1440.

Grimshaw, J. M., Schnemann, H. J., Burgers, J., Cruz, A. A., Heffner, J., Metersky, M., & Cook, D. (2012). Disseminating and Implementing Guidelines. *Proceedings of the American Thoracic Society, 9*(5), 298– 303.

Institute of Medicine (IOM), Committee on Quality of Health Care in America. (2000). To Err is Human: Building a Safer Health System (2000). Institute of Medicine (US) Kohn LT, Corrigan JM, Donaldson MS, editors. Washington (DC): National Academies Press (US); 2000. DOI 10.17226/9728. Retrieved from https://www.nap.edu/catalog/9728/to-err-is-human-building-a-safer-health-system

Institute of Medicine (IOM), Committee on Quality of Health Care in America. (2001). Crossing the Quality Chasm (2001). Washington (DC) National Academy Press, ISBN 978-0-309-07280-9, DOI 10.17226/10027. Retrieved from http://nap.edu/10027

Kirkpatrick, D. L., & Kirkpatrick, J. D. (2006). *Evaluating Training Programs: The Four Levels* (3rd ed.). San Francisco, CA: Berrett-Koehler Publishers.

Kang, J., & Seomun, G. (2018). Evaluating Web-Based Nursing Education's Effects: A Systematic Review and Meta-Analysis. *Western Journal of Nursing Research, 40*(11), 1677 –1697. doi: 10.1177/0193945917729160

Lamb, R. L., Annetta, L., Firestone, J., & Etopio, E. (2018). A meta-analysis with examination of moderators of student cognition, affect, and learning outcomes while using serious educational games, serious games, and simulations. *Computers in Human Behavior, 80*(2018), 158e167.

Lioce, L. (Ed.). (2020). *Healthcare simulation dictionary* (2nd ed.). AHRQ (Agency for Healthcare Research and Quality). https://doi.org/10.23970/simulationv2

McGaghie, M. C., Issenberg, B., Petrusa, R. R., & Scalese, R. J. (2016). Revisiting 'A critical review of simulation-based medical education research: 2003–2009'. *Medical Education, 50*, 986–991. doi: 10.1111/medu.1279

Mikkelsen, J., Reime, M. H., & Harris, A. K. (2008). Nursing students' learning of managing crossinfections – Scenario-based simulation training versus study groups. *Nurse Education Today, 28*, 664–671.

MRSA-veilederen. (2009). *Nasjonal veileder for å forebygge spredning av meticillinresistente Staphylococcus aureus (MRSA) i helseinstitusjoner Nasjonalt folkehelseinstitutt og Helsedirektoratet.* Retrieved from https://www.fhi.no/globalassets/dokumenterfiler/rapporter/2009-og-eldre/mrsa-veilederen.pdf

National Centre for Bilotechnology Information (NCBI). (2016). What are clinical guidelines? Retrievd from https://www.ncbi.nlm.nih.gov/books/NBK390308

Nyameino, J., Rabbi, F., Ebbesvik, B-R., Were, M.C., & Lamo, Y. (2019). A model driven approach to the development of gamified interactive clinical practice guidelines. *Proceedings of the 14th International Conference on Evaluation of Novel Approaches to Software Engineering, {ENASE} 2019, Heraklion, Crete, Greece, May 4-5, 2019*, 147-158 05. SciTePress 2019. ISBN 978-989-758-375-9.

Oculus Integrations. (2020). https://developer.oculus.com/downloads/package/unity-integration/

Reed, S., Shell, R., Kassis, K., Tataglia, K., Wallihan, R., Smith, K., Hurtubise, L., Martin, B., Ledford, C., Bradbury, S., Bernstein, H., & Mahan, J. D. (2014). Applying Adult Learning Practices in Medical Education. *Current Problems in Pediatric and Adolescent Health Care, 44*, 170-181. https://doi.org/10.1016/j.cppeds.2014.01.008

Riel, M. (2000). Education in the 21st Century: Just-in-Time Learning or Learning Communities. In Emirates Center for Strategic Studies and Research (Ed.), *Education and the Arab World: Challenges of the next millennium* (pp. 137-160). Abu Dhabi: Emirates Center for Strategic Studies and Research.

RIVM XXX (Institute for Public Health and the Environment, Epidemiology and Surveillance, 3720 BA Bilthoven, The Netherlands). https://www.rivm.nl/sites/default/files/201905/52238 WHO CAESAR 2018 maps_Part6.pdf

Ruscio, F., Bjørnholt, J., Leegaard, T., Moen, A.E.F., & De Blasio, B. (2017). MRSA infections in Norway: A study of the temporal evolution, 2006-2015. *PLOS ONE, 12*, e0179771.

Sackett, D. L.,. Rosenberg, W. M., Gray, J. A., Haynes, R. B, & Richardson, W. S. (1996). Evidence based medicine: what it is and what it isn't. *BMJ, 312*(7023), 71–72. doi:10.1136/bmj.312.7023.7

Shekelle, P. (2020). Overview of clinical practice guidelines. In M. D Aronson, & J. Givens (Eds.), *UptoDate*. Mar 2020., updated: Apr 08, 2020. Retrievd from https://www.uptodate.com/contents/overview-of-clinical-practice-guidelines

Shiffman, R. N., Michel, G., Essaihi, A., & Thornquist, E. (2004). Bridging the Guideline Implementation Gap: A Systematic, Document-Centered Approach to Guideline Implementation. *J Am Med Inform Assoc, 11*(5), 418–426.

SteamVR. (2020). https://valvesoftware.github.io/steamvr_unity_plugin/

Subhash, S., & Cudney, E. A. (2018). Gamified learning in higher education: A systematic review of the literature. *Computers in Human Behavior, 87*, 192-206. doi. 10.1016/j.chb.2018.05.028

Taylor, D. C. M., & Hamdy, H. (2013). Adult learning theories: Implications for learning and teaching in medical education, AMEE Guide No 83. *Medical Teacher, 35*(11), e1561- e1572. doi 10.3109/0142159X.2013.828153

Unity Game Engine (2020). Unity Technologies. https://unity.com

Unity XR Interaction Toolkit (2020). https://docs.unity3d.com/Packages/com.unity.xr.interaction.toolkit@0.9

Human and Artificial Intelligence for the Society of the Future
Short Paper Book of the European Distance and E-Learning Network (EDEN)
2020 Annual Conference | Timisoara, 22-24 June, 2020
ISBN 978-615-5511-28-8

ERASMUS+ CBHE PROJECT "ENHANCEMENT OF LIFELONG LEARNING IN BELARUS"

Eduard Pavlysh, VSU (Vitebsk State Univesity) named after P.M. Masherov,
Yury Kalesnik, Sukhoi State Technical University of Gomel, Belarus

Abstract

The presentation specifies the overall aim and specific objectives. It is stressed that the project aims to develop and enhance lifelong learning in Belarus with effective use of distance learning & Bologna instruments for the advancement of the regional labour market by developing an inter-University cooperation in the regions in Belarus based on integrating 6 leading regional Universities into an Inter-University Network for Lifelong Learning (ILN); training university managerial and teaching staff for the ILN network using the EU partners' practices; designing, developing, and piloting 5 new on-line (blended) LLL study courses in English, IT, Energy Saving, Entrepreneurship, Financial and Law Literacy to the general public; evaluating the piloted courses and making upgrades.

Besides the three major results – the Inter-University Network for LLL (ILN), 5 new on-line (blended) courses for general public, and making upgrades on the courses – the project has produced a series of effects: (a) modular approach to learning design by Belarusian staff, (b) student-centred education through course design application, (c) varying types/methodologies of assessing students' progress, (d) use of IT-based technology for learning design, (e) orientation to individual learning pathways, and (f) stronger focus on Quality Assurance instruments and procedures.

The presentation also provides statistics of enrolment and graduation from the 5 courses at the 6 partner institutions in Belarus and a plan for sustaining the project's results after the end of the EU funding.

Human and Artificial Intelligence for the Society of the Future
Short Paper Book of the European Distance and E-Learning Network (EDEN)
2020 Annual Conference | Timisoara, 22-24 June, 2020
ISBN 978-615-5511-28-8

THE VR@SCHOOL PROJECT: ABOUT A POWERFUL TECHNOLOGY THAT COULD CHANGE HOW WE LEARN FOREVER

Anca Colibaba, Grigore T.Popa University Iasi/EuroEd Foundation, Romania, Irina Gheorghiu, Albert-Ludwigs University Freiburg, Germany, Ovidiu Ursa, Iuliu Hatieganu University Cluj-Napoca, Romania, Carmen Antonita, Scoala EuroEd Iasi, Romania, Anais Colibaba, Trinity College Dublin, Ireland

Abstract

The article is a study of the VR@School project (Erasmus+ programme), developed within a partnership of schools, education and ICT institutions from Italy, Lithuania, Portugal and Romania. The VR@School project promotes professional development by enabling teachers to use VR technologies and providing them with online educational resources in their classes. The article introduces the project's objectives, outputs and activities. It gives insights into the Teacher's Guide on how to create and use Virtual Reality (VR) and education laboratories in schools to stimulate motivation, student participation in constructing knowledge as well as students' inquiry and problem-solving skills. The aim of the guide is to open up teachers to the use of VR technologies in their classes by offering them a ready-made collection of online tools and platforms to facilitate the teaching/learning process and attract students to become more motivated and involved in learning. The paper also presents the main findings of the survey carried out on a group of teachers from Iasi, Romania, who participated in the project's training course on the Guide. The testimonials collected from teachers give some insights into the new teaching/ learning experience.

European context and the VR project

The unprecedented advance of technology has brought about innovative changes in our society and new demands schools are required to meet. As a result, there is a growing interest in integrating technology into classes, updating school curriculum and bringing education closer to the world of work (Cochrane, 2016). VR offers students rich contextual learning experiences. It simulates reality and enables students' immersion in an experience perceived through their senses. Students get engaged in the experiential learning process where they can apply the new concept learned to a real-world situation, analyse and evaluate it. As students feel and live the experience everything is memorable and easy to retain (Slavova & Mu, 2018; Bardi, 2019; Schechter, 2018).

The VR@School project promotes a new concept in educational technology which is much closer to students' liking: Virtual and Augmented Reality. In today's digital world, Virtual Reality can become an innovation and an added value in school education; it can deliver experiences and interactions for students that are either not practical or not possible in the real world (VR@School project, 2020).

The VR project

Objectives, target groups, methodology and outputs

The European VR project is an illustration of how schools can use technology for the benefit of their students. The European VR project is an illustration of how schools can use technology to the benefits of their students.

The European VR project aims at: encouraging teachers to use up-to-date technologies and online educational resources in their classes by offering them a ready-made collection of online tools and platforms to facilitate the teaching process and attract pupils to become more motivated and involved in learning; training teachers to use the Virtual and Augmented Reality in the classroom; developing VR lesson plans for science subjects and transversal topics (motivation to study/ job orientation, CLIL, inclusive education and prevention of school dropout).

The partnership is made up of high schools ("Grigore Moisil" Computer Science High School, Iaşi, Romania, LT VET School, CIPAT VET School, Italy), nongovernmental organisations in the field of education (EuroEd, Romania, SIH, Lithuania, Pixel, Italy), IT companies (Birouri Vii, Romania; IPB, Portugal) from four countries (Romania, Italy, Portugal, Lithuania).

The project's partnership has created a Teach@School Online Library - Educational Technology and Open Education Resources (a database of resources and useful tips as to how to use them) and a teachers' guide on Virtual Reality in school education with six modules.

The teachers' guide on Virtual Reality in school education

Module 1 highlights the benefits and difficulties of integrating technology into the educational process. The module aims at describing the necessary elements for integrating technology into the classroom, the relation between the current technologies and education, the role of the teacher and a brief history and evolution of WWW.

Module 2 provides information on important topics meant to enhance the teaching and learning processes: Virtual Learning Environments, Personal Learning Environment, Virtual Reality and Augmented Reality. Module 3 provides some insight into the possibilities brought by virtual reality technology for the development and use of VR learning experiences.

Module 4 provides detailed information on the most recent and the most widely exploited teaching methodologies: collaborative learning, experience-based learning and storytelling. Moreover, this module describes how those teaching methodologies can be further improved and enhanced by the use of virtual and augmented reality.

Module 5 provides information about the use of virtual reality in education and ways to create resources while Module 6 focuses on the methods and principles of virtual learning (VR@School project, 2020).

The VR training course

Twenty teachers of scientific school objects (16) and foreign languages (4) from three high schools in Iasi, Romania participated in the VR training course. It is important to mention that no one has ever done a VR lesson or had previous experience with this methodology. The teachers were recruited according to their availability and interest in VR. They were familiarized with the method and state-of-the-art digital tools. The focus of the course fell on devising a template of the VR lesson. Everybody agreed that what makes a VR lesson different from the other lessons is that students get immersed in the environment by using VR, an invaluable experience. Students should be encouraged to explore the scene on their own at first and later on under guidance to find out as much as possible about the topic. Students should be familiarized with VR and its safety rules if it is first introduced. Each time before going to VR, students should be warned about the possible negative effects some of them can get and told they can choose to opt out of VR.

Teachers' feedback

The questionnaires

Teachers' questionnaire (Table 1) had six yes/ no questions asking them to assess their perception and feelings about the course. They also had to describe the challenges and benefits of the method (teachers) and report on what they liked or disliked about the course.

Table 1: Teachers' questionnaire

Question	YES/ NO
1. Was the training course on VR informative and useful?	
2. Was the content clear and easy to follow?	

3. Did the Modules have enough examples and practical applications?
4. Did the training course help you to improve your competences in the use of technology and VR in education?
5. Do you consider that it is difficult to prepare your lessons using VR?
6. Would you recommend the use of VR in the classroom to your colleagues?

Questionnaire results and analysis

The teachers' feedback shows clear strengths of using VR in the classroom. 80% of teachers found the course informative and useful. Most of them (85%) appreciated the content as clear and easy to follow and 65% held that the Modules have enough examples and practical applications. 70% believed that the training course helped them to improve their competences in the use of technology and VR in education. As for how difficult it is to prepare a VR lesson, 50% thought that it could be difficult for them to deliver such a lesson considering the VR video they have to produce. All of them would recommend the use of VR in the classroom to their colleagues considering the impact it has on students' participation in the classes.

All teachers agreed that "Virtual reality can be used to support teaching and learning". To support their view they expressed a lot of arguments: "VR, which simulates reality, immerses the students in an experience perceived through their senses. By raising emotions, excitement, and curiosity the learning experience engages and motivates students, improving learning and making it memorable. The learning material becomes accessible, comprehensible and easy to retain".

VR provides contextual learning experience (similar to lifelike experience). All teachers agreed that "VR helps students relate academic concepts to their own experiences and make connections between new knowledge and experiences they have had. VR uses contextualized learning principles". "Abstract ideas are explained and clarified by practical applications through the process of discovering, reinforcing, and relating. VR enables students to make connections, experience and apply new concepts to their realities. Everything is retained and integrated into the students' learning framework because it is realistic and relevant to the students' life".

The participants also held that "VR encourages cooperation among learners; learning is enhanced through sharing, responding, and communicating with other students. It helps students understand and learn a concept and connect it with the real world". VR provides optimal opportunities for the training of practical skills (linking school with the world of work).

Some teachers highlighted that by using VR in their classes they gain new knowledge and acquire new teaching methods, skills, and techniques, improve their professional profile, their English language, and IT skills. VR also creates "opportunities for teachers to share their best practices, ideas, and materials with colleagues within the EU. They can participate in projects and programs fostering international cooperation and thus, acquire new techniques and ideas which will strengthen their professional profile".

Most teachers believed that education has always relied on interpersonal connections and communication. On the other hand, virtual reality focuses on the software and its user. Therefore if VR is not used wisely, it can affect students' interpersonal relationships and communication. Moreover, some teachers (40%) said that when it comes to technology, there is always the chance that something may get wrong, which will compromise the whole learning process. 45% of teachers complained that their students may also get addicted to the virtual world. Some teachers (35%) were worried about their students getting dizzy or even having headaches because of immersion experiences. Other main concerns were related to the costs of cutting-edge technology, which limits its integration into the whole education system.

The teachers' opinions about the use of VR in classes were favourable. They are in line with other international surveys which evaluated teachers' perception of VR in the classroom[7]. Surveys generally show that teachers support the use of digital technologies in schools and recognize their potential and that there is "sufficient proof that VR can be beneficial in the learning process" (Nadan et al., 2004; Samsung Newsroom, 2017; Slavova, 2018). Although VR is available in a small number of schools, teachers are willing to use it. By using VR teachers demonstrate that they consider what society expects of schools in terms of the demands imposed by the state-of-the-art technology: to continuously upgrade their knowledge, skills and understanding so that they are effective in their work.

Conclusions

Although the study has some limitations in terms of the small number of participants and the short length of the experiment (limited by the project's application), the results are favourable. They show that Virtual Reality provides an unparalleled way to immerse and captivate students. VR offers memorable learning experiences in schools. The teachers highlighted two main reasons which make VR be taken into consideration: experience facilitates learners' retention of knowledge and students are interested in new technologies.

All teachers agreed that VR has benefits: students' better engagement and motivation, enhanced knowledge retention, and decreased "time to learn". VR can give students new ways to experience learning and even create their own media. However, they also held that "implementing the VR methodology requires further training and support". Future work will involve a study focusing on implementing VR in their schools.

References

Bardi, J. (2019, March 26). What is virtual reality? MAXENT 3D COMMERCE [Blog post]. Retrieved from https://www.marxentlabs.com/what-is-virtual-reality/

Cochrane, T. (2016). Mobile VR in education: From the fringe to the mainstream. *Int. J. Mob. Blended Learn. (IJMBL), 8*, 44–60. Retrieved from https://www.igi-global.com/article/mobile-vr-ineducation/163900

Nadan, T., Alexandrov, V., Jamieson, R., & Watson, K. (2004). Is virtual reality a memorable experience in an educational context? *International Journal of Emerging Technologies in Learning (iJET), 6*(1), 53-57. Kassel, Germany: International Association of Online Engineering. Retrieved from https://www.learntechlib.org/p/44953/

Samsung Newsroom. (2017, February 17). Survey Shows that Teachers See Potential for Virtual Reality in Education. Retrieved from https://news.samsung.com/global/survey-shows-that-teachers-see-potential-for-virtual-reality-in-education

Schechter, S. (2018, December 20). 5 top augmented reality and virtual reality technology trends for 2019. MAXENT 3D COMMERCE [Blog post]. Retrieved from https://www.marxentlabs.com/trends-augmented-reality-virtual-2019/

Slavova, Y., & Mu, M. (2018). A comparative study of the learning outcomes and experience of VR in education. *Proceedings of the 2018 IEEE Conference on Virtual Reality and 3D User Interfaces (VR), Reutlingen, Germany, 18–22 March 2018*, 685–686. Retrieved from https://ieeexplore.ieee.org/abstract/document/8446486

Vr@school Project. (2020). Retrieved from https://www.vr-school.eu

Acknowledgments

The paper is a study of the VR@School project (2018-1-RO01-KA201-049411), which is developed under the Programme: Erasmus+, Key Action: Cooperation for innovation and the exchange of good practices in the field of Strategic Partnerships for school education.

Human and Artificial Intelligence for the Society of the Future
Short Paper Book of the European Distance and E-Learning Network (EDEN)
2020 Annual Conference | Timisoara, 22-24 June, 2020
ISBN 978-615-5511-28-8

THE INHIBITORS AND ENABLERS AFFECTING THE ONLINE BEHAVIOURS OF ONLINE COLLEGE STUDENTS LEARNING IN A BLENDED LEARNING CONTEXT

Sharon Rolé, University of Malta, Malta

Abstract

This paper portrays part of a larger study which explores the new online collaborative learning experiences of a class of thirty-seven college students learning in a blended learning context. The research is a case-study with a multi-method interpretivist approach using observations, unsolicited meetings, VLE tracking system, students' reflective journal, online informal discussions, questionnaires, focus groups and individual interviews. This paper focuses on the experiences of students as described in their own voice. It briefly describes the online journeys and identifies the online challenges faced by these students. Although 86% of the students were familiar with the Internet and computers, six online complex behaviour patterns emerged. The findings indicated that the enablers and inhibitors affecting the learners' online behaviours were of a situational, infrastructural and persona-related nature. Situational factors are due to the learner's lifestyle. Infrastructural factors are external factors that are not directly under the control of the learners, whereas the persona-related factors are characteristics of the learners' personalities. This work is of great significance in contexts of novice online learners and of cases where educators shift from traditional face-to-face learning to blended or online learning.

Introduction

The study discussed in this paper is part of a larger study which was an inquiry into factors affecting the online learning experiences of A-level chemistry students studying in a blended learning course in a college in Malta and the impact of these experiences on learning identity (Rolé, 2014). The research questions which directed this part of the study were (a) what were the online behaviour patterns of the learners following a blended course?, and (b) what factors influenced online behaviours in a blended learning context? The students in this study experienced an innovative mode of learning which involved changes from traditional face-to-face learning to blended learning and from an individualistic mode of learning to collaborative learning.

Garrison and Vaughan (2008) describe blended learning "as the thoughtful fusion" of face-to-face and online experiences. The blended learning environment in this research was based on the supplemental model, where the traditional face-to-face meetings are maintained and supplemented with out-of-class online activities via a virtual learning environment (VLE). Teenagers are often described as digitally literate, connected, immediate, experiential and social (Oblinger & Oblinger, 2005). However, several studies e.g., Jefferies et al. (2006), Sweeney et al. (2004) show that in general, college and university students resist the use of technology for study. Studies have shown that the majority of Internet users make use of the Internet to access information and to communicate via social networking and not to participate in content creation activities (Bennett & Maton, 2010).

Several researchers presented models to explain students' resistant behaviours. Garland (1993) modified Rubenson's (1986) model and categorised barriers to online learning into situational, institutional, epistemological and dispositional barriers. Berge and Huang (2004) categorised the factors into three variables: personal, institutional and circumstantial. Berge and Muilenburg (2005) identified eight influencing factors, which listed in order of priority with the most critical first are - social interactions, administrative and instructor issues, learner motivation, time and support for studies, technical problems, cost and access to the Internet, technical skills, and academic skills.

Methodology – Practitioner Research

As a practitioner I designed, implemented and conducted a blended learning course with students who were accustomed to traditional face-to-face learning based on an individualistic and ritualised approach (Boaler & Greeno, 2000). The online work which complemented the learning in the face-to-face class covered all nine topics in first year advanced level chemistry syllabus. Most online work was based on a socio-constructive approach to learning and included the use of wikis, discussion fora, glossary and lab simulation tasks, which were accessed from the virtual learning environment (VLE) Moodle 4.1. As a researcher, I designed and implemented a multi-method interpretivistic research inquiry to explore the students' response to the innovative online learning. The main study (Table 1) was carried out during 34 weeks in the academic year 2007-2008, and this was preceded by a four-month exploratory study in the previous year 2006 -2007, with a different cohort of college students.

Table 1 indicates the data generating methods and the period when the research method was employed. A zooming-in approach (Nisbet & Watt, 1984) was used to allow (a) an insight of online collaborative learning as experienced by all the students in the class, and (b) a focus on a resilient group of twelve students. The generated data was stored, coded, categorised several times, reduced and analysed using the qualitative analysis software Nvivo 8. The intense coding and repeated categorisations of the data gave me a deep understanding of the students' experiences of online participation. The findings from the final whole class individual and the in-depth interviews with the resilient students were treated as primary data. This data was triangulated with the other generated data (weeks 1-24) (see Table 1).

Table 1: Data generating methods and the time frame for data collection. (Rolé 2014, 2020)

Week	Tool/ Research method	Data
< 1	Questionnaire 1 (Q1): student profile questionnaire	Students' familiarity with technology
1-28	Unsolicited face-to-face chats with students	Students' thoughts on course activities
1-32	Researcher's journal	Observation, reflections and development of ideas.
1-32	Virtual Learning Environment tracking system	Students' access and engagement in the VLE.
1-2	Informal online fora (Ice –breaker activities)	Students' perceptions of online learning and collaborative learning.
5	Student's reflective journal	Reflections on some online activities.
7	Questionnaire 2 (Q2): early stages questionnaire	Students' developed attitude towards course.
8	Two ad-hoc group interviews	Purposeful selection of non-participating students
16	Questionnaire 3 (Q3): Middle Stages questionnaire	Functioning of groups and the students' roles
23-24	Two focus group meetings	Students' perceptions and experiences.
28-34	23 Individual interviews; 12 in-depth interviews	Students' perceptions and experiences.

Findings and Discussion

This section is divided in two parts. The first part provides the context for the main findings reported in this paper.

The challenges for online learning and the online journeys

Data collected from the profile questionnaire (Q1) showed that all 37 students in the class (25 females and 12 males) had a computer and Internet connection at home. Six students indicated a reluctance to use computers for study. All students used e-mail, 86% were Internet users and 80% used social networks. The data also revealed a general increase in engagement in the VLE and in collaborative learning as the course progressed. Analysis of the data revealed that the learners were facing three sequential challenges to become successful online learners, namely, (a) the acceptance of online learning as a learning method, (b) the ability to use the computer, Internet and VLE tools and (c) the ability to be a self-directed learner and to contribute to online collaborative activities. A diversity in online student behaviour patterns emerged and six student behaviour groups were identified (Figure 1). For easy reference, these were likened to terms selected from music dynamics – Marcato (emphatic), Moderato (moderate speed), Crescendo (becomes louder), Diminuendo (becomes softer), Staccato (detached) and Ritenuto (held back). One enthusiastic student who was an innovator and a knowledge mediator was the only Marcato (Route 1). He participated in all activities and met all three challenges. The Crescendo students (Route 5 & 6, n = 12) were the resilient students and late adopters who eventually met all challenges. The Moderato students (Route 4, n = 9) participated in small group work but not in whole class discussions. The Diminuendo students (Routes 2 & 3, n = 4) were late rejecters of online learning. The Staccato students (Route 7, n = 7) participated in few online activities The Ritenuto students (Route 8, n = 4) were early rejecters. The Marcato, Moderato and Crescendo students formed the active online learning community of 22 students in the last term.

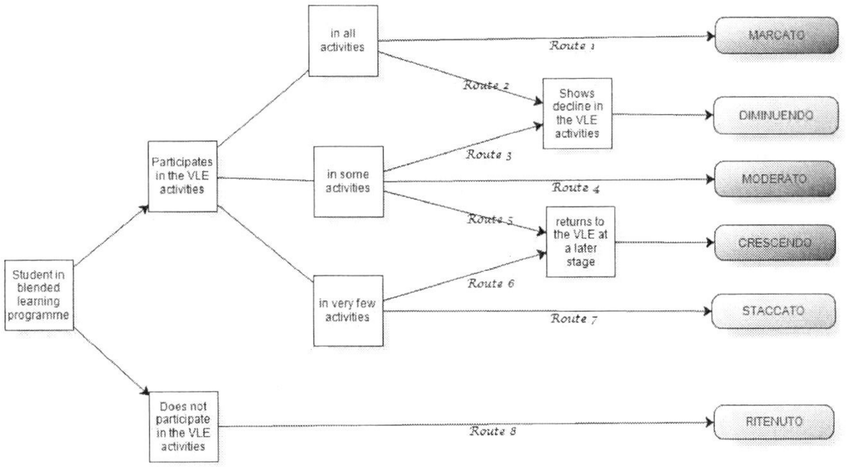

Figure 1. The online behaviour patterns (Rolé, 2014, 2020)

The factors (inhibitors and enablers) which influenced the online behaviours

Data generating methods (Weeks 1 – 24)

The three questionnaires gave a general understanding of the student experiences. The ad-hoc and focus group meetings clarified issues and were instrumental for students to reflect on their experiences. Several issues emerged in the responses in the anonymous middle stages questionnaires and in the focus group meetings. This may be explained by the fact that by this time, there was an increase in the number of students who gained trust and hence showed a willingness to voice their concerns and likes. Analysis of the data emerging from the first 24 weeks in the research was primarily categorized as personal, technological and social issues (Table 2).

Table 2: Issues emerging from data generated up to Week 24 (Rolé, 2014)

Personal Issues	Technological issues	Social issues
Shyness	Unfamiliarity with VLE use	Post work at a late stage
Discouragement: accumulation of incomplete tasks	Computer used frequently by other family members	No communication with others in group
Fear of missing on examinable content	VLE is time consuming	No contribution of work to group
Fear of appearing non-knowledgeable	Fear of using technology	Group conflicts re division of work
Lack of confidence in subject matter	Computer in noisy area at home	Uneasiness to edit work of others
Nothing to add to postings	Time limit on Internet use (costly dial-up system)	Lack of confidence in work of others (*P)
Lack of interest to use the VLE	Time limit on computer use (by parents)	Discussing each others' work is time consuming
Internet for recreation	VLE is tedious to use	Some members dominate the group
Preference for use of pen and pencil	Outdated computer	Preference for individual work (*P)
Lack of time to use the VLE	Low connectivity	
Keen to give support in whole-class discussion		
Assess their learning		
Learning through observation		
Liked PowerPoint presentations		
Self-confident and self-disciplined		

24 Interviews plus 12 In-depth interviews with the resilient Crescendo students (Weeks 28 – 34)

The individual interviews afforded a richer picture of the students' experiences in their own voices. These confirmed, expanded upon and triangulated the initial data. The new rich data necessitated a framework of different categories. I extended Garland's (1993) framework of inhibitors as a model to suit my data of inhibitors and enablers. These factors were categorised in three main themes – situational, infrastructural and persona-related.

Table 3: A framework of the factors affecting online participation (Rolé, 2014)

	Inhibitors and Enablers	
Situational	Infrastructural	Persona-related
Time-management	Institutional	Epistemological beliefs
Online learning/VLE issues	Outside college settings	Personal states
Experiential		Computer use skills
Out-of-class opportunities		Learning dispositions

Situational inhibitors

These were due to the personal choices (Stanford-Bowers, 2008) and unless the students themselves were prepared to change their lifestyle, they could not be able to meet the challenges. This was the case with the Diminuendo (4), Staccato (7) and the Ritenuto (4) students. Five Crescendo students were also affected by situational barriers, but these students were able to overcome their situational problems. These inhibitors included:

- *Time-management issues*: These affected students who were involved in part-time employment, social work, attended extracurricular activities or who missed had personal issues due to illness or familial problems.
- *Online learning related issues*: These affected students who considered online work as unnecessary or as optional or who associated the Internet with leisure and playing games. Three Crescendo and four Staccato students who were familiar with the Internet referred to the VLE interface as "strange", "odd", "complicated" or "different".
- *Experiential issues*: These included the past and ongoing negative experiences of collaborative learning, e.g., "Our *group was a disaster, no one started any work. When I tried, I had no response" (Crescendo 1, Focus group)*
- *Out-of-class opportunities*: These affected two Ritenuto students who lost interest in learning chemistry in both the face-to-face class and also in the online medium. These students were waiting for an opportunity to attend another course in another institution

Infrastructural inhibitors

These were both institutional barriers and home limitations to the access of computers and the Internet. These factors affected six Crescendo, one Moderato and four Staccato students.

- *Institutional issues* presented constraints beyond the control of the learner. Technology such as computers and wireless local area networks were unavailable in the classroom. Students did not find time to visit the college's IT department due to heavy lecture time-tables and unavailability of the labs at several periods. .
- *Outside college settings* refer to home limitations such as poor Internet connectivity, outdated computers, time-restricted Internet connections, computer failures and restricted use of computers at home. Two Staccato students complained of non-ideal working spaces at home due to the computer being used by other family members and placed in noisy common areas.

Persona-related factors

These are factors which were somehow under the control of the student.

- *The students' epistemological beliefs regarding self-directed learning and collaborative learning:* Data analysis revealed that several students started the online course with an understanding of acquiring knowledge, rather than individually or collaboratively constructing it. The data generated from the interviews confirmed that the two predominating epistemological beliefs were (a) learning occurs when knowledge is transferred from the teacher to students (n = 19), and (b) collaborative learning is not as effective and efficient for learning (n = 14).

> *"In Moodle there are students with different styles of expressing themselves. I am afraid I get confused. I would want to have one set of good notes from the teacher and use them to pass my exams" (Crescendo 2, in-depth interviews)*

> *"I preferred to present my own work and get marks for my own effort. I feared that in the group I had to settle for some of the work which was not good enough" (Crescendo 3, in-depth interviews)*

- *Personal states:* These included cyber phobia, shyness and a lack of self-confidence in contributing to class discussions.

> *"I am too embarrassed to take part. The questions they ask make me feel like I live in the moon because I don't understand them, so I feel useless because I cannot help them either. I am very shy. It is embarrassing" (Crescendo 4, individual interviews)*

- *Online reflective and writing skills:* Some students experienced an inability to reflect on tasks and write when using a computer. Some others found it difficult and tedious to write chemistry text with the keyboard.
- *Online learning dispositions:* Learning dispositions are described by Claxton and Carr (2004) as the readiness and the willingness to learn. The data analysis revealed that the Marcato, Crescendo and Moderato students had these four key online learning dispositions: resourcefulness, resilience, reciprocity and responsibility (Rolé, 2014; 2020), which were developed.

Resourcefulness: The disposition of resourcefulness focuses on the cognitive aspects of learning and was indicated by (a) a curiosity about online learning and an academic curiosity, (b) a confidence in the new learning design, in the teacher and in them self as a learner, and (c) a flexibility in the appropriate use of different resources. The learning disposition of resourcefulness is essential for traditional students to become self-directed and collaborative learners. The students who were knowledge mediators in the active learning community, had this disposition.

Resilience: This disposition focuses on the emotional aspects of learning and was exhibited by the active learners both at the macro level, in terms of using online learning as a learning method and also at the micro level, where online learners persisted to solve chemistry problems. The twelve Crescendo students had a disposition to be resilient and despite the inhibiting factors which caused setbacks and frustrations (Juutinen & Saariluoma, 2010), they persisted and eventually met all the online challenges.

Reciprocity: This disposition focuses on the social dimension of learning and promotes student learning through active engagement and a socio-constructive approach to learning. Students, who lacked this disposition, were unable to cope with the third challenge. Successful online participation of the 22 students who formed an online learning community depended on the possession of this disposition or its development through observation and imitation (Duncan, Jones, & Carr, 2008)

Responsibility: This disposition, which focusses on the moral aspect of learning, was shown when a student took responsibility for one's own learning and when a student took responsibility for the learning of others. In the first case, this disposition was crucial for learners to become self-directed learners and develop self-regulatory and resource management skills. In the second case, the disposition was crucial for collaboration and community formation. Palloff and Pratt (2003) remarked on the robustness, breadth and richness of the disposition of responsibility. They stated that students who take the opportunities to become responsible learners are empowered to move to other learning experiences with an even greater sense of responsibility and accomplishment. This was shown by some of the students when they became responsible students supporting each other's learning also in the face-to-face environment.

> *"I see what problems other students have. I was not always able to solve problems, but I used to do some research, so that first I understand the concepts well and then I help the others; and I could tell how well I knew the topic myself" (Marcato, individual interviews)*

Conclusion

This study looked at the barriers and enablers of online learning. Situational inhibitors can be overcome if the students change their lifestyle. The infrastructural factors are not directly under the control of the learners and the persona-related factors are characteristics of the students. The Crescendo students showed that negative factors such as epistemological beliefs associated with traditional learning can change. The learning dispositions of resourcefulness, resilience, reciprocity and responsibility are the dispositional pillars of online collaborative participation. Online learning dispositions can be developed through observation and imitation. The positive factors discussed in this paper were the forces which produced an active online learning community composed of help seekers and knowledge mediators. A shift in student roles from passive learners to help-seekers to knowledge mediators became evident as the course progressed.

Implications for practice

This research has produced a framework of student online behaviours and a framework of factors which affect online participation. These frameworks are of great use as analytical or diagnostic tools for teachers conducting blended learning courses. Teachers engaged in blended learning will be able to understand and use the above framework (Figure 1) to be aware of and to be prepared for various online student behaviours. For example, the Crescendo students did not immediately engage with online participation. Thus teachers will be ready to support such students, by creating the right conditions for their learning. The framework displaying the factors affecting online participation is useful as both an analytical tool to help teachers understand the various factors which inhibit or enable online participation, and also as a diagnostic tool which can be used to support students. For example, infrastructural factors which inhibit participation need to be addressed at an early stage of the course. This research has shown that although some students confirmed that they had Internet access at home, in reality they were unable to work online due to connectivity or computer availability problems. The tool enables the teacher to be prepared to counteract the barriers to online learning. The teachers can then consider ways of motivating and encouraging student participation. For example, one barrier to online participation, which teachers might not expect to find, is the unwillingness of active Internet users to use technology for study purposes.

This work is of great significance in situations such as the Covid-19 pandemic period, where several educators have switched to online learning and even more so in post Covid-19 pandemic period, where as currently predicted, there will be a large shift in learning from the traditional face-to-face to blended learning.

References

Bennett, S., & Maton, K. (2010). Beyond the 'Digital Natives' debate: towards a more nuanced understanding of students' technology experiences. In S. De Freitas, & J. Jameson (Eds.), *The e-learning reader* (pp.135-146). London: Continuum.

Berge, Z. L., & Huang, Y. (2004). A model for sustainable student retention: a holistic perspective on the student dropout problem with special attention to e-learning. *Deonews, 13*(5). http://www.ed.psu.edu/acsde/deos/deosnews/deosnews13_5.pdf

Berge, Z. L., & Muilenburg, L. (2005). Student barriers to online learning: a factor analytic study. *Distance Education, 26*(1), 29-48. Retrieved from https://pantherfile.uwm.edu/simonec/public/Motivation retention articles/Articles/Muilenberg_StudentBarriersToOnlineLearning.pdf

Boaler, J., & Greeno, J. G. (2000). Identity, agency and knowing in Mathematics Worlds. In J. Boaler (Ed). *Multiple perspectives on mathematics teaching and learning* (pp.171-200). Westport: Ablex.

Claxton, G., & Carr, M. (2004). A framework for teaching learning: the dynamics of disposition. *Early Years, 24*, 87-97.

Duncan, J., Jones, C., & Carr, M. (2008). Learning dispositions and the role of mutual engagement: factors for consideration in educational settings. *Contemporary Issues in Early Childhood, 9*(2), 107-117.

Garland, M. R. (1993). Student perceptions of the situational, institutional, dispositional and epistemological barriers to persistence. *Distance Education, 14*,181-198.

Garrison, D. R., & Vaughan, N. D. (2008). *Blended learning in higher education: framework, principles and guidelines.* San Francisco, CA: Jossey-Bass.

Jefferies, A., Quadri, N., & Kornbrot, D. (2006, June). New generation learners: does the learning environment match student expectations? *First Annual Blended Learning Conference.* University of Hertfordshire, Hatfield. http://uhra.herts.ac.uk/bitstream/handle/2299/6102/901863.pdf?sequence=1

Juutinen, S., & Saariluoma, P. (2010) Emotional obstacles for e-learning: a user psychological analysis. European Journal of Open, Distance and E-learning (EURODL), 2010(1). Retrieved from https://www.eurodl.org/materials/contrib/2010/Juutinen_Saariluoma.pdf

Nisbet, J., & Watt, J. (1984). Case Study. In J. Bell, T. Bush, A. Fox, J. Goodey, & S. Goulding (Eds.), *Conducting small scale investigations in Educational Management* (79-92). London: Harper and Row.

Oblinger, D. G., & Oblinger, J. L. (Eds.) (2005). *Educating the Net generation.* http://www.educause.edu/ir/library/pdf/pub7101.pdf

Palloff, R. M., & Pratt, K. (2003). *The virtual student: a profile and guide to working with online learners.* San Francisco, CA: Jossey-Bass.

Rolé, S. (2014). *An inquiry into factors affecting the online learning experiences of A-level chemistry students studying in a blended learning course in a college in Malta and the impact of these experiences on learning identity* (Doctoral thesis). The University of Nottingham. Nottingham UK. http://eprints.nottingham.ac.uk/14511/

Rolé, S. (2020, February). The identification of key online learning dispositions of college students studying in a blended learning course. *3rd International Conference on Research in Education, Teaching and Learning (ICETL)*, Rome. Retrieved from https://www.dpublication.com/wp-content/uploads/2020/02/688-521.pdf

Rubenson, K. (1986). Distance education for adults: old and new barriers for participation. In G .Van Enckevort, K. Harry, P. Morin, & H.G. Schutze (Eds.), *Distance higher education and the adult learner: innovations in distance education* (pp. 39-55). Heerlen, Netherlands: Dutch Open University.

Stanford-Bowers, D. E. (2008). Persistence in online classes: a study of perceptions among community college stakeholders. *MERLOT Journal of Online Learning and Teaching, 4*(1), 37–50.

Sweeney, J., O'Donoghue, T., & Whitehead, C. (2004). Traditional face-to-face and web-based tutorials: a study of university students' perspectives on the roles of tutorial participants. *Teaching in Higher Education, 9*(3), 311-323.

Human and Artificial Intelligence for the Society of the Future
Short Paper Book of the European Distance and E-Learning Network (EDEN)
2020 Annual Conference | Timisoara, 22-24 June, 2020
ISBN 978-615-5511-28-8

OPEN VIRTUAL MOBILITY BETWEEN STUDENT TEACHERS FROM ITALY AND SPAIN: AN OPPORTUNITY FOR THE ENHANCEMENT OF THE CURRICULUM

Antonella Poce, Roma Tre University, Italy, Gemma Tur, University of the Balearic Islands, Spain, Francesca Amenduni, Roma Tre University, Italy, Antònia Darder, University of the Balearic Islands, Spain

Abstract

Virtual Mobility is a challenging learning design to promote international collaborative work among students in Higher Education. It meets the requirements of HE to become more international, digital and at the same time, flexible and democratic. In order to give student teachers a VM experience, a team of lecturers of Teacher Education programs from the RomaTre University (Rome, Italy) and the University of the Balearic Islands (Balearic Islands, Spain) agreed to work in open digital environment. Students were asked to create, in groups from the two countries, Open Digital Resources (OER) in which they plan how to work in international online contexts with their future students. This article reports on the learning design and explores the technological tools they envisioned along with their general satisfaction. Conclusions reflect on further improvements for new editions of the activity.

Introduction

Higher Education is facing the challenge of the globalization and digitalization that current society is requiring (Buchem, Tur, & Urbina, 2018). In order to answer to both challenges, the uptake of Virtual Mobility (VM) could emerge as an option for HE institutions. Furthermore, Ruiz Corbella and Garcia Aretio (2010) have argued that VM helps in the democratization of HE as more students have access to a wider institutional market as well as brings greater interactivity and flexibility for the affordances of the technological tools in which it is based. The concept of Virtual Mobility has been defined as "a set of ICT supported activities, organized at institutional level, which realize or facilitate international, collaborative experiences in a context of teaching and/or learning" (Op de Beeck & Van Petegem, 2013; Poce, Amenduni, Re, & De Medio, 2020). While most of early experiences may have been institutionally supported and could have been based on previous formal learning agreements, the current project challenges what is previously known by opening up Virtual Mobility. In this regard, the new emergent concept of Open

Virtual Mobility is understood as extending the potential of open digital environments for VM and at the same time extending the contexts from more to less formalized agreements among Higher Education institutions, teachers and students. Thus, agency of the learner is enhanced by choosing where, what and how to learn.

Firssova and Rajagopal (2018, 15-19) have researched about the skills involved in open virtual mobility, and they list the following seven along with an eighth area of knowledge:

- Intercultural skills and attitude: gaining cultural knowledge, understanding cultural perspectives, enhancing own cultural identity, enhancing cultural understanding, demonstrating cultural understanding, applying intercultural awareness in culturally challenging circumstances.
- Interactive and collaborative learning in authentic international environments: enhanced teamwork skills, collaborating with peers from different discipline, collaborating with peers within the context of an international learning experience, interacting with authentic international resources in a foreign language.
- Autonomy-driven learning: Demonstrating self-directedness in decision-making on own learning, Demonstrating independent learning.
- Networked learning: engaging in digital networking, dealing with complexity in networked learning.
- Media and digital literacy: Demonstrating learner control, being proficient in using online learning technologies, Being proficient in assessing quality in courses and resources found online.
- Active self-regulated learning skills: Being able to self-regulate learning processes, Being able to self-reflect on learning experiences, Demonstrating ownership over own learning (attitude).
- Open-mindedness: Being open- minded and tolerant, demonstrating self-confidence in interaction with peers and teaching staff, Show willingness to improve proficiency in foreign languages.
- Gaining Knowledge of Virtual Mobility: Understanding Virtual Mobility, Understanding Open Education.

In VM activities the technological environment is both very important and a challenge (Bassani & Buchem, 2019) and this is particular interesting in case of student teachers who need good early experiences to use as reference for their future teaching careers.

The Virtual Mobility activity

The learning activity was designed between the two teams of lecturers from the two participating Universities: Roma Tre University (Rome, Italy) and the University of the Balearic Islands (Balearic Islands, Spain). The two teams had arranged to share a common design with common learning objectives and activities that could be embedded in the curriculum of the different subjects involved. As a first iteration of the design, the assessment stage was carried out locally and a separated stage from the development of the common activity.

Participants

There were more than 500 students involved in both the international contexts. In Spain there were a total of 240 students, involved in five groups, which were allocated in the three locations of the UIB: in the main campus in Palma (Mallorca) and in the off-campus centres in Ibiza and Menorca. Students from the UIB were doing a subject on ICT for Primary Education in the third year of the Teacher Education program. In Italy 30 students took part in the virtual mobility activity from two university courses, named respectively "Educational Research Methodology" (18 students) and "Museum, Experiment and Reading" (12 students). Students from the "Educational Research Methodology" course were at the first year of their Teacher Education program whilst students from the "Museum, Experiment and Reading" course were at their fourth year. There were seven lecturers involved in the activity from the two locations. From the total of students, 52 finally chose participate in the virtual mobility exchange activity.

Table 1: Description of participants

1	Total of groups	Total of programs	Total of students	Total of participants	Total of male students	Total of female students
Roma Tre	is		289	30	3	27
UIB	5	1	206	22	6	16

The total number of 52 students who chose to participate in the virtual mobility activity were teamed up randomly by lecturers into eight groups, with three or four students from each international context. Before selecting the activity, students were given the information of the learning design, in particular, the educational aims and the tasks and outcomes that would be expected from them.

The learning design

The activity was designed to promote the following four learning objectives: knowing the concepts of virtual mobility and virtual exchange; exploring collaborative work environments and tools; creating open educational objects; networking with other future teachers from international contexts; and, developing students collaborative skills;

The learning design was based on a didactic sequences of three key moments:

- Beginning. Starting with the concept of virtual mobility, and in particular, in a proposal for collaborative work in international contexts.
- Application. Working collaboratively with students from the University of Rome3 (Italy).
- Closing. Individual reflection on the activity developed and the learning achieved.

Based on the didactic sequence, the following tasks and along with recommendations and instructions were given to students of both contexts:

- From the two recommended readings (Bassani & Buchem, 2019; Ruiz Corbella & García Aretio, 2011), make the Introduction to the concepts of virtual mobility and virtual exchange, as different modalities of meetings in virtual environments among students of different contexts. In particular, see the possibilities of virtual exchanges for collaborative work with Primary Education students.
- The UIB's teaching staff formed the groups and prepare a list with names and emails.
- The group of students of the UIB works collaboratively with the group of students of the Roma3 University. The context of the activity is described as follows (Table 2):

Table 2: The context of the activity

"You are invited to participate in an international project with Italian/Spanish teachers and plan a collaborative task for primary school students from Italy and Spain. Students should be enabled to work collaboratively around the cultural heritage of their city (for example, Rome and Palma / Menorca / Eivissa). Before working with your primary school students, you are required to decide with teachers from another country which collaborative tools are suitable for your purpose. The following steps are recommended: 1. Please, contact the Italian and Spanish colleagues by email to make the first suggestions and arrange an appointment through Skype; 2. Select three tools before the meeting (tools for creating content in a collaborative way such as presentations, posters or other multimedia objects for Primary Education, taking into account the tools you have worked in the workshop Multimedia tools and resources added in the final list); 3. During the virtual meeting with Italian/Spanish colleagues discuss about the three tools you chose (1 hour) 4. Work together in a presentation on Google Drive. Include four tools for collaborative work with Elementary students. Add the CC license for the presentation; 5. Add an individual slide highlighting what you liked most and what you learned from the foreigner students; 6. Maintain communication with Italian/Spanish students during the process to make decisions about common work. Optionally, you can meet again with your international partners to conclude the presentation.

Regarding this sequence, the VM activity was developed in the tasks during the application stage whereas the beginning was developed separately in each local context. The reflective task had to be included in the common OER as artefact to be submitted.

To introduce the teams in which students had been joint randomly, and to promote communication among each member, the activity was started with an email from the two lecturers who were coordinating the activity. The initial task of presentation needed an extended deadline to compensate initial misunderstandings. The emails were written in three languages (English, Italian and Spanish), from which we present the versions in English:

Table 3: Emails sent by lecturers

	Text of the email
First email Introduction	Welcome to your exchange international group between University of Roma Tre and University of the Balearic Island. Attached you can find the names' list of the member of your group. The first task that we wish to ask you is to introduce yourself to your group. Your presentation should include: - your name and surname; your age; your field of study; your interests and hobbies; your motivation to join the activity. - If you want, you can also add the links to your Social Media profiles (e.g. Facebook, LinkedIn, Twitter and Instagram) in order to create "digital bonds" with the members of your group. Please, introduce yourself before the 17th October. To organise the Skype meeting, optionally, we suggest to use Doodle, in which one of you should set up a range of dates so everyone chooses when they are available.
Second email Reminder	Dear students, Thank you for sharing your presentations with the members of your group. If you didn't do it yet, we ask you to introduce yourself not later than the 20th of October. Otherwise, it would be not possible to participate in the next steps of the activity. Attached you can find the calendar with the next activities you will be required to complete within your group. Enjoy your weekend Your teachers
Third email	Dear students, We did not receive your presentations. Without your presentations, it is not possible to participate in the exchange. Did you do your presentations through private emails? If yes, please include always us in the communication because we need to monitor your work. Please forward us your presentations if you did it in other communication. I need an answer from you before tomorrow at 12 am. If I do not receive any email from each of you, you will be excluded from the exchange activities. Looking forward to hearing from you. Best regards,

Students were free to organize their time and tasks as they considered suitable, but also they were suggested the following schedule:

Table 4: Recommended schedule

	Recommendation
Week 1 10-17 October	Introduce yourself to your colleagues in the group
Week 1bis 18-20 October	Last days for students who haven't done their presentation
Week 2 21-27 October	Prepare the meeting with your classmates (prepare the tools you can recommend) Negotiate the date for the meeting Share the tools you would recommend
Week 3 28 oct- 3 November	Meet and take decisions on the tools you want to include Start the work on the joint presentation
Week 4 4-10 November	Work on the presentation
Week 5 11-15 November	Add your own slides of your self-assessment on the learning you have experienced through working with others Last editions and submission

Research

The current study is aimed at exploring the development of the Open Virtual Mobility activity. Two research questions guide our study:

- What tools do students include in their designs and which of them involve curriculum enhancement?
- What is the level of satisfaction among students?

To answer the first question, an analysis of content will be carried out. For the first research question, a list of technological tools and collaborative environments along with their learning designs will be done. For the second one, the general satisfaction will be explored with a Likert-scale question that students answered among others in the institutional survey on the diverse learning activities they carried out.

Results

The analysis of the content in students OER allows us to list the collaborative and technological environment that students envision in their designs. The following table (Table 5) describes which tools were included in the OERs collaboratively created by Roma Tre and UIB students. For this information, we highlight which ones were in previous design of the syllabus in each local university, and therefore, which were new and involve the enhancement of curriculum.

Table 5: Curriculum enhancement due to the Open VM activity. (I for RomaTre, Italy and S for UIB, Spain)

	Included in Curriculum	Enhanced curriculum
Google Drive	S; I;	
Explain everything		S; I
Canva	S	I
Story Jumper	S	I
Storybird	S	I
Edmodo	S	
Mindmester	S	
Mural.ly	S	I
Stomboard		S; I
Google MyMaps	S	I
Google Art & Culture		S; I
Eduloc	S	I
Kahoot	S	I
Google Glass	S	I
Movie Maker	S	I;
Prezi	S	
Enhanced book	S	I
Tapsy		S; I
Tux Paint		S; I
Padlet	S; I;	
Minecraft education	I	S
Steller		S; I
Podcast	S	I
Skype	I	S
Virtual Reality Headset		S; I
Total Italy	4	12
Total Spain	16	9

As showed in table 5, the eight groups included in total 25 tools in their OERs. Most of the tools they included in their 8 OERs correspond to the ones presented in the both curricula (N = 18). However, they introduced 7 tools not included in both the curriculum. These results suggested that students did not only share their respective knowledge about tools, but they also looked for new tools during the collaborative international group-works.

As for the second research question, we tried to see if students were satisfied about the learning experience, and if it could have helped them for further learning. In the Italian context, most of the students (N = 13) showed general satisfaction and only 1 student fully disagree with the statement and 5 students were neutral.

Data shows that students at the UIB were not satisfied in general. The total answers from level 3 to level 5 (totally in agreement) show that 65% of students were generally satisfied. However, the 35% of students clearly unsatisfied and the 35% of students who only reported partial satisfaction allows us to observe important limitations in the implementation of the activity. Comments by students show problems of organization, for example, difficulties to coordinate schedules, highly influenced by local routines and habits, and confusions with the aims of the work along with different ways of managing teamwork. collaborative and technological skills in other group activities throughout the course. As presented in the following graphic.

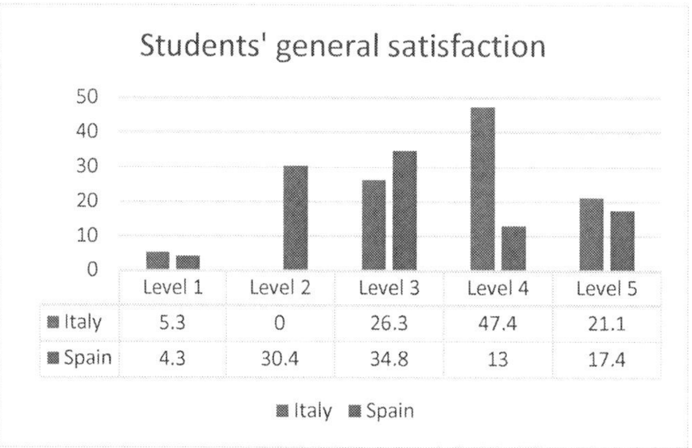

	Level 1	Level 2	Level 3	Level 4	Level 5
Italy	5.3	0	26.3	47.4	21.1
Spain	4.3	30.4	34.8	13	17.4

Graphic 1. General satisfaction of participating students in the Open Virtual Mobility activity

In the Italian context, we tried to understand if the Virtual Mobility activity helped students to generalize their 8 students strongly agree and 6 agree with the statement "We have collaborated through the use of different technologies in the following activities". Only 2 students disagree with the previous statement and 3 were neutral.

Discussion and conclusion

As for the first research question, the designs with a wide variety of tools by students involve the enhancement of the curriculum in each University. In this sense, as for the total of 25 tools named by students, 12 of them were new for the program in RomaTre whereas 9 of them were not previously included in the subject syllabus at the UIB.

Virtual mobility is an approach for the development of skills between HE students in different countries. However, it could be argued that VM has a special interest in Teacher Education so future teachers can live experiences with peers abroad and envision how to work in international contexts with their future students in projects such as the eTwinning, which is related to non-HE institutions. Regarding the research questions, it can be confirmed that the curriculum of both contexts have been enhanced by the VM learning activity. As for the second research question, although students were generally satisfied, there is a rather relevant amount of students expressing some disagreement.

The lessons learned during this first iteration of the Open VM activity between Roma Tre and the UIB allow us to bear in mind the following suggestions and improvements: an online common session with students from both contexts; sharing a Virtual Learning Environment., in which students can communicate and share with lecturers at the same time; and lecturers can track students' work and help and give feedback based on students' evidence; include in the task the evidence of the meetings and their agreements; and, add an online session in which students may be able to present their work

References

Bassani, P., & Buchem, I. (2019). Virtual exchanges in higher education: developing intercultural skills of students across borders through online collaboration. *RIITE. Revista Interuniversitaria de Investigación en Tecnología Educativa, 6*, 22-3. doi:10.6018/riite.377771

Buchem, I., Tur, G., & Urbina, S. (2018). Quality assurance for attainment, assessment and recognition of virtual mobility skills in context of open education. QA Framework in the Open Virtual Mobility project. Edulearn Conference 2-4 July 2018. Retrieved from https://iated.org/concrete3/view_abstract.php?paper_id=65036

Firssova, O., & Rajagopal, K. (2018). Open VM Competence Framework. Retrieved from https://www.openvirtualmobility.eu/topics/outputs

Ruiz Corbella, M., & Garcia Aretio, L. (2010). Movilidad virtual en la educación superior: ¿oportunidad o utopía? *Revista Española de Pedagogía, 246*, 243-260. Retrieved from https://reunir.unir.net/bitstream/handle/123456789/3854/MovilidadVirtualEnLaEducacionSuperior.pdf?sequence=1&isAllowed=y

Op de Beeck, I., & Van Petegem, W. (2013). Virtual mobility: an alternative or complement to physical mobility? *ERACON 2011 & 2012 Dual Year Proceedings*, 151-160.

Poce, A., Amenduni, F., Re, M., & De Medio, C. (2020). Assessing a MOOC users experience in a virtual mobility project: preliminary results for quality enhancement. *Italian Journal of Educational Technology.*

Acknowledgements and Disclaimer

Acknowledgements: This paper is based on the joint work and research conducted by partner organisations in the Erasmus+ Project Open Virtual Mobility, Cooperation for Innovation and the Exchange of Good Practices, Strategic Partnerships for higher education, (partially) founded by the European Union, Project Number 2017-1-DE01-KA203-003494.

Disclaimer: The creation of these resources has been (partially) funded by the ERASMUS+ grant program of the European Union under grant no. 2017-1-DE01-KA203-003494.

Neither the European Commission nor the project's national funding agency DAAD are responsible for the content or liable for any losses or damage resulting from the use of these resources.

ISBN 978-615-5511-28-8

README – RESEARCH PROPOSAL TO DEVELOP OPEN EDUCATIONAL RESOURCES FOR EDUCATIONAL IMPROVEMENTS

Cristine Martins Gomes de Gusmão, Secretaria de Programas de Educação Aberta e Digital – Universidade Federal de Pernambuco, Carlos Alberto Pereira de Oliveira, Instituto Multidisciplinar de Formação Humana com Tecnologias – Universidade do Estado do Rio de Janeiro, Patrícia Smith Cavalcante, Secretaria de Programas de Educação Aberta e Digital – Universidade Federal de Pernambuco, Brazil

Abstract

Nowadays digital curation involves maintaining, preserving and adding value to digital research data throughout its life cycle. Therefore, the active management of research data reduces threats to its long-term value and mitigates the risk of digital obsolescence. Meanwhile, objects (materials, content, products, data, processes) safeguarded in trusted digital repositories can be shared among the broader research community. This proposal deals with the need to create an Open Educational Resources (OER) at the Federal University of Pernambuco (UFPE) in view of the great development of academic-scientific materials and products to face COVID-19. This paper aims to present an ongoing research to support the development of REAdME an Open Educational Resource.

Introduction

In the face of global actions to support the fight against the coronavirus pandemic, and consequently, COVID-19, many initiatives have been created, products and processes developed and under development. In Brazil it is no different, as well as at the Federal University of Pernambuco (UFPE). An initiative of great importance and interest is available to the community and society through the Covid-19 Observatory.

This observatory encompasses research projects associated with different themes that integrate strategic actions in four areas: diagnosis and identification, public policies, economics, society and creative industries.

In view of the wealth of ongoing investigations (Markauskaite & Goodyear, 2018), materials and products of the highest quality that are being and will be developed, the purpose of the Open Educational Resource developed for Academic Improvement (REAdME) is to present and make available these resources (materials, products, processes) worldwide. Unique learning that can help, not only at the present moment, but also in similar future situations.

The use of open educational resources (OER) is a worldwide trend, extremely reinforced by the context currently experienced (Caballé et al, 2014; Mason & Lefrere, 2003). Positive impact related to the creation of an institutional OER, especially with information about Covid-19, is the visibility of the scientific and academic reference of great value, nationally and internationally.

This proposal aims to develop the OER model for UFPE considering what is already developed and under development and conduct research (Silva et al., 2006) on the solutions made available at the Covid-19 Observatory to suggest adjustments of the materials and products generated, to the shape of the objects that can be made available in the REAdME.

After this introduction the paper is structured as follows. The second section presents the specific goals. Section three make the methodology defined available and Section four brings some expected outcomes. At the end considerations are made.

Specific Goals

Given the proposal and the defined objective, specific objectives were described to better achieve the expected results.

1. Identify and describe the OER model, as well as a technological platform, developed and used by UFPE, for academic documents;
2. Model the OER structure to receive educational objects (materials, products, models and processes) generated during the pandemic period by professors, researchers and professors at UFPE;
    a. Proposal a Sustainable Model
3. Investigate at the Covid-19 Observatory and other UFPE projects, in accordance with the essential requirements of the pandemic, to make the various products under development available through financing;
4. Develop policy and guidance for licensing, making available, using and remixing resources made available in REAdME.

Materials and Methods

To contemplate the general objective and specific objectives foreseen, the technical team will use technological mediation for investigations and meetings, during the COVID-19 pandemic, Table 1 present related tasks. The main activities are:

- Research on reference models and approaches inherent to the development of Open Educational Resources, in line with current regulations and models recommended by the literature and UNESCO Recommendations (Markauskaite & Goodyear, 2018; Fergunson et al, 2017; Butcher et al., 2015).
- Study the materials and objects previously developed and made available at the COVID-19 Observatory – identify important characteristics and requirements of the products and propose a set of metadata.
- Study the sustainable development objectives of Agenda 2030, define categories and analysed all projects initially catalogued in the thematic axes were reassessed in the perspective of the SDGs.

Table 3: Phases for develop the REAdME OER

Phase	Activity	Outcomes
Seek	Bibliographical research and material of interest on OER, including that developed at the Federal University of Pernambuco (UFPE). UNESCO recommendations.	Technical report of what have been developed at UFPE. Important requirements for modelling REAdME. Product: Report with the findings and preliminary view of the model to be developed.
Understand	Analysis of projects versus products expected from the Covid-19 Observatory and other initiatives by UFPE professors / researchers	List of products and display of objects to be made available. Product: Updated version of the report.
Refine	Analysis of documents generated so far and refine the model	Product: Model Report updated. Description of the proposed OER Model – REAdME.
REAdME	Detailing of technical documentation – Policy, guidelines (license, availability, use, remixing).	Products: (a) Policy to make teaching, learning or research materials available in the public domain or openly licensed, in order to allow their use, reuse or adaptation by third parties. (b) Intellectual property license guidelines that define the terms of use, adaptation and distribution of content by third parties.

Expected Results

From the application point of view, the expected results with this project have a special impact on the availability of scientific and academic material and products (Bourkoukou et al., 2017; Caballé et al., 2014; Silva et al., 2006; Mason & Lefrere, 2003), through definition and modelling, in an Open Educational Resources (OER) repository.

The parameters that will integrate the REAdME Open Access Policy, will be based on the Brazilian copyright law, to guarantee that the educational resources of REAdME can be disseminated and reused freely, by anyone, whether in educational activities for self-learning or use. In the daily practice of professionals in the specific areas provided. List of manuals (guidelines and policies) that will be developed and will guide the use of REAdME:

- Terms of use – document that will present and specify how the educational resources assigned with the signature of UFPE's Copyright Assignment Term and made available in the Open Educational Resources Collection developed for Educational Improvement (REAdME) can be used.
- REAdME development policy – UFPE's REAdME Access Policy establishes guidelines to guarantee access, use and reuse of educational content, respecting the author's moral rights.
- Filling manual – technical sheet with metadata.
- Copyright regime – copyright guide.

Final Considerations and Current Situation

The Federal University of Pernambuco (UFPE) has expanded its offer of online courses since 2007, some specializations and online courses. In order to tackle the COVID-19 pandemic, it is important that most postgraduate and graduate courses have as many online classes as possible, and in parallel, many R&D resources and calls to foundations have been launched across the world. Addressing these opportunities, many projects and proposals have been approved and products are being developed.

Attentive to this type of production, UFPE is concerned with the quality of its production. As many teachers do not know, or are not used to or do not believe in the potential of digital education and are not qualified to participate in this type of work (Welsh et al., 2003), the biggest challenge faced so far are: composition of the qualified team to plan and implement the development of available products digitally, in that sense, OER has emerged as a concept with great potential to support this educational transformation.

References

Bourkoukou, O., Elbachari, E., & Eladnani, M. (2017). A Recommender Model in E-learning Environment. *Arabian Journal for Science and Engineering, 42*(2), 607-617.

Butcher, N., Kanwar, A., & Uvalic-Trumbic, S. (2015). *A Basic guide to open educational resources (OER).* UNESCO. Retrieved from https://unesdoc.unesco.org/ark:/48223/pf0000215804

Caballé, S., Gañán, D., Gómez, M., Conesa, J., Rius, A., & Santanach, F. (2014). Experiences at the Open University of Catalonia with the Virtualization of Live Collaborative Learning in Support for Engineering Education. *International Journal of Engineering Education, 30*(3), 663-674.

Ferguson, R., Barzilai, S., Ben-zvi, D., Chinn, C. A., Herodotou, C., Hod, Y., Kali, Y., Kukulska-Hulme, A., Kupermintz, H., McAndrew, P., Rienties, B., Sagy, O., Scanlon, E., Sharples, M., Weller, M., & Whitelock, D. (2017). *Innovating Pedagogy 2017: Open University Innovation Report 6.* Milton Keynes, UK: The Open University.

Markauskaite, L., & Goodyear, P. (2018). *Universities should take stronger leadership on knowledge and how it matters.* University of Sidney. Retrieved from https://theconversation.com/universities-should-take-stronger-leadership-on-knowledge-and-how-it-matters-89849

Mason, J., & Lefrere, P. (2003). Trust, collaboration, e-learning and organisational transformation. *International Journal of Training and Development, 7*(4), 259-270.

Silva, J., Ramos, L., & Noronha, D. (2006). Base de dados. In Población, D.,Witter, G.,Silva. *Comunicação e produção cientifica: contexto, indicadores, avaliação* (pp. 263-285). São Paulo: Angellara.

Welsh, E., Wanberg, C., Brown, K., & Simmering, M. (2003). E-learning: emerging uses, empirical results and future directions. *International Journal of Training and Development, 7*(4). ISSN 1360-3736

Acknowledgements

The project team thanks the Dean of Research (Pró-Reitoria para Assuntos de Pesquisa e Pós-graduação – Propesq) for the financial support granted for the development of the README Project.

Human and Artificial Intelligence for the Society of the Future
Short Paper Book of the European Distance and E-Learning Network (EDEN)
2020 Annual Conference | Timisoara, 22-24 June, 2020
ISBN 978-615-5511-28-8

INTEGRATING THE LEARNING BY DESIGN PEDAGOGY IN TEACHER TRAINING – TRAINING STEM TEACHERS TO USE VIDEO CONFERENCING WITH AN EXPERT TO DIFFERENTIATE LEARNING PROCESSES

Jonas Bäckelin, M.A. Student at Linköping University, Sweden

Abstract

A professional teacher continuously observes and reflect on the teaching practice and its effect on student learning. The aim of this research project is to integrate the Learning-by-Design pedagogy, when training teachers to use interactive video conferencing in classroom instruction. The outcome will hopefully promote new methods to include assessment for learning in STEM teaching where the teacher becomes a reflective designer of learning experiences. This didactic strategy is also believed to increase engagement of diverse learners and train critical thinking. Another part of the project is to create an online course for teachers that can be included as a training activity in teacher's professional development. The approach for integrated academic development can be overwhelming for in-service teachers. The plan is to design and test a learning activity rubric that describes eight "Knowledge Processes" to foster higher order thinking skills and deeper learning. The final part is to explore learning analytics and educational data mining to make learning expectations explicit along with data visualization of progress.

Introduction

This research project in progress is the final requirement for the international Master program Adult Learning and Global Change (ALGC), offered by the University of Linköping in collaboration with the Canadian University of British Columbia, the South African University of Western Cape and the Australian Monash University (Linköping University, 2020).

STEM subjects are often combined with traditional classroom instruction and school-sanctioned texts, where teachers guide students in decoding and comprehending texts as opposed to critiquing them (Stevens, 2002). Technology Enhanced Learning (TEL) has among other things allowed interactive video conferencing, which can be used to change teacher's classroom instruction. This has been addressed by Grant and Cheon (2007), who wrote "New approaches to instruction must accompany new technologies, adjusting to the changing teacher's role, motivating learners, and preparing learning materials to fit the synchronous conferencing". Since then instruction practices developed for STEM education has been included the science curriculum in several countries (Sanders, 2009), but there is now research emphasising a need to develop new strategies for teaching STEM (Winberg et al., 2018).

The ongoing EU funded project "Integrated Approach to STEM teacher training", involving 10 universities from 4 EU countries and 6 universities from Russia and Kazakhstan, focus on enhancing the quality of STEM Teacher training at partner universities in line with Bologna provisions and needs of knowledge economy (Välimaa & Hoffman, 2008). The model for integrated academic development helps teachers to understand their teaching and its effect on student learning. The project published this information on their webpage as background "Knowledge and skills related to science, technology, engineering and mathematics (STEM) are crucial for sustainable economic development in the 21st century and are becoming an increasingly important part for basic literacy in today's knowledge economy according to the European Schoolnet. Developments in these fields underpin advances in scientific research across all disciplines and drive innovation and job creation across much of world economy" (Erasmus + STEM Project, 2020).

PART 1: New methods to include assessment for learning in STEM teaching

The scope in this much smaller research project is limited to didactic strategies of Learning-by-Design pedagogy in order to promote new methods to include assessment for learning in classroom instruction. In this context the teacher bring diversity into the learning experience and become "teacher-as-designer".

Lesson plans become shareable "designs-for-learning", with different learning pathways and assessment is formative performance in relation to knowledge processes (New Learning Online, 2020). In this part of the project teachers will test a learning activity rubric that describes eight "Knowledge Processes" to foster higher order thinking skills and deeper learning. The 21st Century Learning Design (21CLD) was a professional development program based on rubrics to help teachers design lessons and learning activities (Ulbrick & Smith, 2014). The same methodology is going to be used for the knowledge processes (see Figure 1).

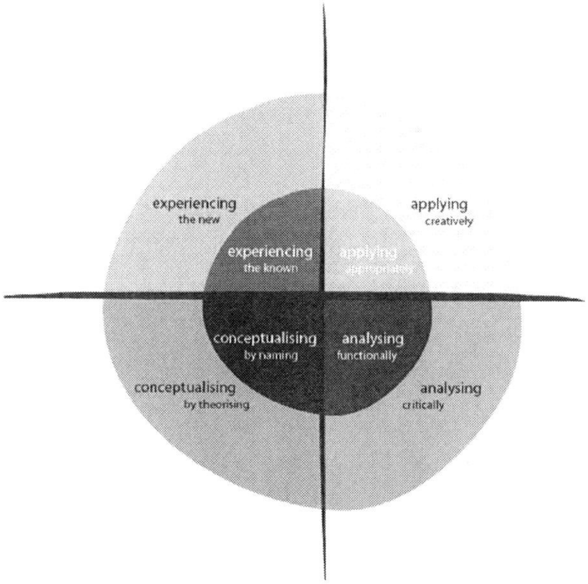

Figure 1. The Learning by Design pedagogy uses eight "Knowledge Processes" multiliteracies (New Learning Online, 2020)

PART 2: Create an online course for teachers

I was one of the first teachers in Sweden to make use of Microsoft's initiative "Skype in the Classroom" (Microsoft, 2020), but already in 2011 there were 13,500 participants worldwide. During the last Global Learning Connection event in 2019 the participants of the community travelled 29 million miles in 48 hours and had participants from more than 110 countries. Today I'm participating in the Skype Master Teacher Program (SMTP) and are registered as a guest speaker on the topic of how Baltic Sea fish populations are affected by fishing, eutrophication and oxygen depletion (Microsoft, 2020a). Digital communication has been highlighted in of the training module for educators in digital competence by the Swedish National Agency for Education. One of the assignments in the first section is to "Plan to conduct a lesson where students use a digital tool to communicate with someone outside the classroom who has expert knowledge of the subject area you are working with" (Skolverket, 2020).

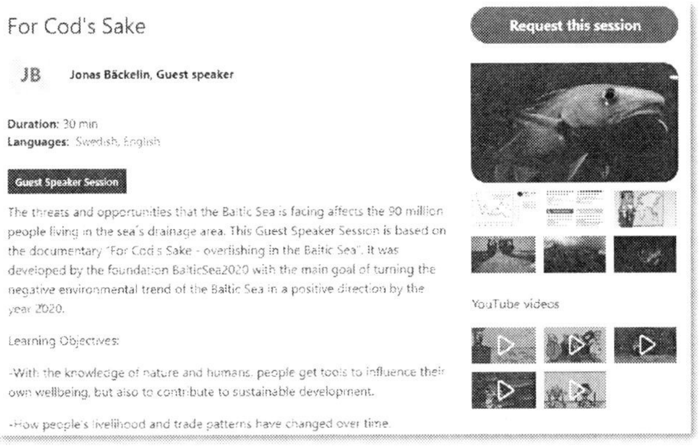

Figure 2. Guest Speaker Session "For Cod's Sake – overfishing in the Baltic Sea" (Microsoft, 2020a)

A virtual interview with an expert situates the subject in the real world. It is important to create a clear learning objective and chunk instruction so students can complete one task at the time. In my research project, I have so far seen several benefits from using the initiative Skype in the Classroom from Microsoft Education. The purpose of the online course is to share best practise for implementation of video conferencing with an expert as a design element in the lesson plan for teachers. The recommendation is to use a video conferencing system that is in line with school policies and an example is Microsoft Teams (see Table 1).

Table 1: Step-by-step guide to help you organize and participate in Skype in the Classroom activities (Microsoft, 2020b).

Tools	Tips
Lobby	Make sure you or the educator monitor and admit participants from lobby into the meeting. You can change the meeting role to presenter role to ensure the educator can moderate during the connection
Introduction	The educator should start the call by saying hello as part of the class greeting and remind students the learning objectives and expectations. Spend 5 minutes in the beginning of the call outlining behaviour and call etiquette you can use the slides in the appendix. You can introduce yourself and the topic of the call.
Screen Sharing	After your introduction, we recommend sharing your screen using a PowerPoint or other visuals in order to lock the presenter window on your content.
Pinning	If you're mainly presenting on camera and not screen sharing, you can instruct the students how to pin you as the main screen. If the student is on the Teams app, they can right click on your image and pin you as the presenter. (Tip: if you really need to lock the view on your webcam for all participants, open your Camera app on your computer and then share your screen.)
Muting Participants	As a presenter, you can mute all. On Microsoft Teams, meetings with more than 5 participants will automatically mute participants to help control noise.
Q&A time	Be ready to call on students or encourage them to type their question in the chat box for you to answer them after the presentation. The "Raise your hand" feature is available in Microsoft Teams.

Part 3: Explore learning analytics and educational data mining

Today learning analytics and educational data mining is offering integral formative assessment that supports and tracks progress. This make learning expectations explicit along with data visualization of progress. It is believed this can be used for structured support in group or peer-to-peer learning and also make it easier for the teacher to manage the logistics of differentiated instruction.

The CG Scholar platform is developed by the Common Ground Media Lab, the research and technology arm of Common Ground Research Networks. CG Scholars new analytics area is a learning visualization tool, where student's unit of work is displayed and the teacher can see the comparative progress of all members of the class, identifying which students may require more time or special attention (CG Scholar, 2020).

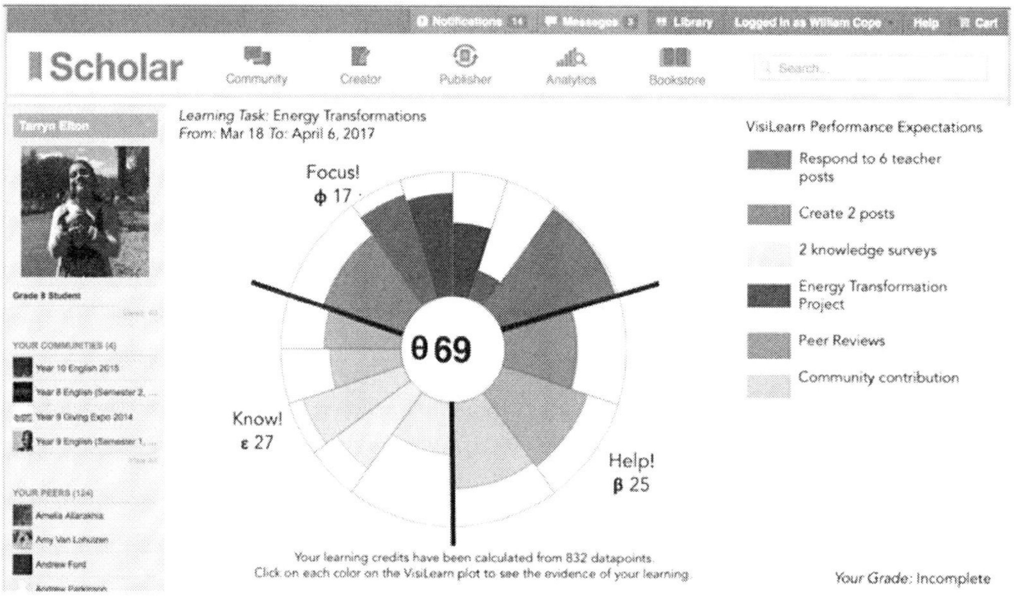

Figure 3. Scholar's new analytics area: Analytics learning progress visualization (CG Scholar, 2020)

I believe this final part of the project is a very important development in order to change the classroom practise for STEM teachers and include assessment for learning. CG Scholar promotes life-embedded learning and the development will soon allow to transform methods for collaborative learning using big data and artificial intelligence. This will probably not be possible to include in the scope of the online course for using video conferencing with an expert, but will certainly be an area of future research.

References

Cope, B., & Kalantzis, M. (2009). "Multiliteracies": New literacies, new learning. *Pedagogies: An international journal, 4*(3), 164-195

CG Scholar. (2020). Scholar's New Analytics App: Towards Mastery Learning. Retrieved May 24, 2020, from https://cgscholar.com/community/community_profiles/new-learning/community_updates/54189

Grant, M. M., & Cheon, J. (2007). The value of using synchronous conferencing for instruction and students. *Journal of Interactive Online Learning, 6*(3), 211-226.

Linköping University. (2020). Master's programme Adult Learning and Global Change. Retrieved May 9, 2020, from https://liu.se/en/education/program/l7mlg

Microsoft (2020). Skype in the Classroom: A free global community that fosters empathy and compassion for each other and our planet. Retrieved May 21, 2020, from https://education.skype.com

Microsoft (2020a). Skype in the Classroom User Page for Jonas Bäckelin. Retrieved May 9, 2020, from https://education.skype.com/u/jonas.backelin

Microsoft (2020b). Guide for Guest Speakers and Content Partners. Retrieved May 10, 2020, from https://education.skype.com/p/guest-speaker-content-partner-guide-remote-learning

New Learning Online. (2020). The Learning by Design pedagogy. Retrieved May 24, 2020, from https://newlearningonline.com/learning-by-design/pedagogy

Sanders, M. (2009). STEM, STEM education, STEMmania. *The Technology Teacher, 68*(4), 20–26.

Skolverket. (2020). Leda och lära i tekniktäta klassrum. Retrieved from Del 1: Moment B – kollegialt arbete May 21, 2020 from https://larportalen.skolverket.se/#/modul/0-digitalisering/Grundskola/201_Leda_och%20_lara_i_tekniktata_klassrum/del_01/

Stevens, L. P. (2002). Making the road by walking: The transition from content area literacy to adolescent literacy. *Literacy Research and Instruction, 41*(3), 267-277.

Ulbrick, R., & Smith, K. (2014). 21st Century learning design: A model of professional learning. *Learning and Teaching, 7*(1), 41-69.

Välimaa, J., & Hoffman, D. (2008). Knowledge society discourse and higher education. *Higher Education, 56*(3), 265-285.

Winberg, C., Wright, J., Wolff, K. E., Pallitt, N., Bozalek, V. G., & Conana, H. (2018). Critical interdisciplinary dialogues: Towards a pedagogy of well-being in stem disciplines and fields. *South African Journal of Higher Education, 32*(6), 270-287.

Human and Artificial Intelligence for the Society of the Future
Short Paper Book of the European Distance and E-Learning Network (EDEN)
2020 Annual Conference | Timisoara, 22-24 June, 2020
ISBN 978-615-5511-28-8

TRANSITIONING A JK-12 INTERNATIONAL SCHOOL FROM BLENDED TO ONLINE LEARNING IN RESPONSE TO AN EXTERNAL SHOCK: LESSONS LEARNED

Julia Tokatlidou, Maria D. Avgerinou, Peggy Pelonis, American Community Schools (ACS) Athens, Greece

Abstract

The COVID-19 pandemic and ensuing school closure in March 2020, perceived as a forced and imminent change, was a problem outside the locus of control of the leadership of ACS Athens, a private, large JK-12 American International school located in Athens, Greece. The school's blended learning culture along with the associated, school-wide, ongoing Action Research were the only constants that could operate as critically enabling factors toward the smooth transition to online learning. While data collection is still underway, in this paper both preliminary results and lessons learned are shared regarding the primary research goal, namely, to systematically and formatively perform an effective evaluation of online teaching and learning experiences in the Elementary, Middle, and High School with the view to improving their design, delivery and outcomes for all involved stakeholders.

Introduction and Theoretical Framework

The American Community Schools (ACS) Athens is a private, large JK-12 American International school located in Athens, Greece. In 2013, the school introduced its learner-centred i^{2}Flex (blended) instructional methodology, which is grounded on social constructivism, and reflects a more inclusive conceptualization of the K-12 blended learning landscape (Avgerinou, Gialamas, & Tsoukia, 2014; Avgerinou & Gialamas, 2016; Avgerinou & Pelonis, 2021). Moodle is the learning platform that facilitates and promotes i^{2}Flex-based learning experiences school-wide. Over the past 7 years, Middle (MS) and High School (HS) teachers have participated in extensive, systematic professional development led by the in-house eLearning expert and a team of faculty with professional interest in educational technology, in order to make the mandatory transition from regular face-to-face (F2F) to blended learning- and for those interested, to online learning (Avgerinou, 2019). Last Fall, virtual HS courses were offered to both students in-house, and worldwide. Throughout this extended period of time, an ongoing, whole-school Action Research (AR) study has been conducted to monitor, evaluate and improve the implementation of blended (and subsequently the online) teaching and learning from Grades 4 and 5 (pre-i²Flex) to Grades 6 through 12.

The instructional design criteria and educational technology frameworks that underpin the i²Flex methodology, guide the design, development and implementation of the ACS Athens Blended and Online Course, and inform the continuous teacher PD and performance evaluation are:

- the Quality Matters (Quality Matters, 2016) course design standards and K-12 rubric which is educational technology research-based;
- the TPACK framework (Mishra & Koehler, 2009; Ward, 2011) that promotes pedagogically sound educational technology integration;
- the Community of Inquiry (CoI) Framework (Garrison, Anderson, & Archer, 2000; Bogle et al., 2009; Boston et al., 2009) that promotes teacher, cognitive, and social presence online.

The COVID-19 Challenge as an Action Research Pivot

The COVID-19 pandemic and ensuing school closure in March 2020, was perceived as a problem outside the locus of control of the school leadership. The blended learning culture along with the associated, ongoing AR were the only constants that could operate as critical enabling factors toward the smooth transition to online learning.

This unprecedented, and (aptly called) Remote Emergency Teaching situation (Hodges et al., 2020) further impacted the existing AR parameters of our study: there was a considerable variation in online teaching experience among the three school principals. The educational leaders of the school led by the President intentionally developed a responsive, formative data-driven strategy with the objective to minimize the psychological negative impact on the students, and to optimize the learning outcomes during this challenging period. The existing AR process assumed now a different pace and turn: data gathering and analysis became part of the leadership's weekly endeavours in order for changes at all levels (e.g. teaching, learning, and logistics interventions) to occur promptly and address issues as effectively as possible in real time.

Research Context

Research Goals/Questions

Our primary research goal was to systematically and formatively perform an effective evaluation of online teaching and learning experiences in the Elementary, Middle, and High School during the COVID-19 period with the view to improving their design, delivery and outcomes for all involved stakeholders (students, teachers, and parents). Our secondary research goals were to evaluate (a) whether and in what ways the leadership and instructional approaches adopted in this period, have effectively addressed the problem and re-established the equilibrium for the entire community, and also (b) whether and to what extent the existing i[2]Flex culture of the school has functioned as a stabilizer, facilitated and expedited its transition to Online Teaching and Learning.

Methodology and Process

With the standing AR framework in place and in anticipation of what might occur, the prospect of school closure was proactively addressed by the President and the educational leadership team mid-February. Adopting a combination of an adaptive yet shaping strategy (Reeves, Haanaes, & Sinha, 2015) for that forced AR intervention, the leadership decided that the objective was to continue the delivery of curriculum without interruptions for the MS and HS by turning the schools to online teaching utilizing the prior experience in blended learning. At that point, needs related to technology infrastructure, teacher and student training for the synchronous/asynchronous sessions were identified and evaluated.

Professional development (PD) on the use of the online platform for synchronous teaching (via Moodle's Big Blue Button/BBB) took place f2f the week before the school closure both for faculty and students, and continued virtually throughout the closure. Online teaching began the day after the school closure, and for the MS/HS it followed a specific schedule with a 40/60% ratio of synchronous/asynchronous sessions. In order to build an effective learning curve for teaching and learning in an online environment, synchronous sessions for those schools were gradually increased per course. For the ES, the process was different due to the fact that neither students nor faculty of grades 1 through 5 had any prior direct experience with blended learning. Still, as Grade 5 was trained on pre-blended learning and had already integrated Moodle in their daily work, it followed the same process as MS and HS. During the first two weeks and given the uncertainty of the length of the closure, for grades 1-4 the objectives were to first give emphasis on the asynchronous learning while reviewing previously taught content, so that students, parents and teachers could shift slowly their mindset and practices towards independent, online learning. After that time, synchronous sessions were introduced and new curriculum was covered.

All departmental leaders reported daily the progress of the Virtual Learning for their departments, the challenges faced and the number of students who had difficulty in reaching the set learning goals. Academic counselling support for learning differences and psychological support was also offered online. The latter was further enhanced with additional individual and group sessions helping students to cope with the COVID-19 anxiety and fears. Further, counselling sessions were also offered to faculty who needed personal and/or family support in coping with similar issues.

Data Collection and Analysis

Formal data was collected through surveys run by the principals' office and the Academic Dean's office. The MS and HS principals surveyed almost weekly faculty and students, while parent surveys went out from the Dean's office. The questionnaire was designed to include both quantitative, and qualitative data through open ended questions, comments and suggestions. In addition, formal data was collected from performance on tests, quizzes, projects, and daily homework. Informal data was gathered through student and parent emails to faculty and the administration, as well as from parent phone calls, PTO meetings, and focus group virtual meetings.

Data analysis is ongoing. Quantitative data has been analysed through descriptive statistics while qualitative data has been undergoing content analysis.

Preliminary Findings

With respect to the main research question, the data derived especially from the surveys indicated a high rate of parent and student satisfaction with the virtual learning experience at ACS Athens and the strategy that has been followed (75%). Student performance data does not differ considerably from that of quarter 1. It should be noted that almost all MS and HS courses included online summative assessments in quarter 3. Curriculum delivery data, at end of the 3rd week, indicate a two-week delay in reaching the planned curriculum delay. The regular pace of curriculum delivery is expected to be resumed once the steep 'learning curve' phase is completed, and with the support of both the additional synchronous sessions, and the overall adjustment to virtual learning.

Data from faculty's satisfaction with the online teaching experience, indicate a smooth transitioning to online teaching despite the fact preparation and actual teaching time online were suddenly much more demanding, as well as anxiety to deliver high quality teaching online was rather high. Student adjustment to the online experience was found to be 35% extremely easy, 46% easy, and 18% easy after the first two days of virtual schooling.

For grades 1 through 4, findings indicate that almost 25% of the parents favour more synchronous sessions that would keep the children engaged all day with their teachers. At the end of the second virtual week, curriculum delivery was approximately 3 weeks behind. Except for homework, there have been no other summative assessment data for grades 1-4. Further, the formative data gathered is not sufficient at this point to evaluate the performance against the standards and benchmarks of the school. More performance data is currently being collected which may indicate a considerably steeper, yet expected student learning curve in the online environment.

Lessons Learned Thus Far

The gradual approach in achieving the right balance between asynchronous and synchronous teaching driven by feedback from faculty, students and parents helped in continuing teaching and learning without major disruptions. As a result, the school community's equilibrium was swiftly re-established.

Faculty PD right before and throughout the school closure regarding both educational technology tools, and online learning designs, has clearly supported the smooth transition of faculty to the new teaching mode. Different types of PD (group, grade, one-to-one) have addressed diverse teaching needs as thoroughly as possible. This is in line with what Archambault et al. (2014) have proposed for online teachers who "need to have not only an excellent grasp of their given content area but also an appreciation of how technology and the online environment affect the content and the pedagogy of what they are attempting to teach" (p. 87).

The opportunities for virtual social gatherings during the country's lockdown, the offering of psychological support to faculty as needed, the considerate approach of the educational leaders fostered a positive professional environment and strengthen the feeling of belonging to the community. As a result, more opportunities for collaboration among faculty were observed which supported better student learning.

The existing i^2Flex school culture and all prior training aiming at the development of the requisite soft and technology skills, has been identified as one of the main reasons of the rather seamless transition of HS and MS to online teaching learning. The lack of prior i^2Flex training of the ES inhibited the timely transition to online teaching and learning. Indeed, synchronous teaching could have started much earlier had ES faculty been exposed to the i^2Flex methodology along with their colleagues from HS and MS. Yet, the fact all faculty PD for the past seven years was intensely focused on blended teaching and thus a related school culture organically emerged, seemed to have eased ES teachers preconceived concerns and challenges with educational technology, and consequently assisted them in developing skills and techniques for age appropriate technology-enhanced teaching. As a result, they displayed a high level of adaptability, grit and resilience when they were called to teach online, and in a sense "build the plane while flying it".

Finally, the approach taken for the faculty PD, the data-driven decisions, and the frequent and systematic communication with the parents were crucial in maintaining the community spirit strong during crisis, and in making the transition to online successful for all stakeholders.

References

Archambault, L., Debruler, K., & Freidhoff, J. R. (2014). K-12 online and blended teacher licensure: Striking a balance between policy and preparedness. *Journal of Technology and Teacher Education, 22*(1), 83–106.

Avgerinou, M. D. (2019). The architect inside (will eventually connect the dots). In C.T Miller & A.A. Piña (Eds.), *Lessons in Leadership in the Field of Educational Technology* (pp. 129-140). Springer.

Avgerinou, M. D., & Gialamas, S.P. (Eds.). (2016). *Revolutionizing K-12 blended learning through the i2Flex classroom model.* Hershey, PA: IGI Global.

Avgerinou, M. D., Gialamas, S., & Tsoukia, L. (2014). i2Flex: The meeting point of web-based educa- tion and innovative leadership in a K-12 international school setting. In D.G. Sampson, D. Ifenthaler, J.M. Spector, & P. Isaias (Eds.), *Digital systems for open access to formal and informal learning* (pp. 329-344). New York: Springer.

Avgerinou, M. D., & Pelonis, P. (Eds.). (2021- forthcoming). *Transforming K-12 Blended and Virtual Learning Through the i²Flex Classroom Model.* Hershey, PA: IGI Global.

Bogle, L., Cook, V., Day, D., & Swan, K. (2009). Blended program development: Applying the Quality Matters and Community of Inquiry Frameworks to ensure high quality design and implementation. *Journal of the Research Center for Educational Technology, 5*(2), 51–66. Retrieved from http://www.rcetj.org/index.php/rcetj/article/viewArticle/3

Boston, W., Diaz, S. R., Gibson, A. M., Ice, P., Richardson, J., & Swan, K. (2009). An exploration of the relationship between indicators of the Community of Inquiry framework and retention in online programs. *Journal of Asynchronous Learning Networks, 13*(3), 67–83.

Garrison, D. R., Anderson, T., & Archer, W. (2000). Critical inquiry in a text-based environment: Computer conferencing in higher education. *The Internet and Higher Education, 2*(2–3), 87–105.

Hodges, C., Moore, S., Lockee, B., Trust, T., & Bond, A. (2020, March 27). The difference between emergency remote teaching and online learning. EducauseReview [Blog post]. Retrieved from https://er.educause.edu/articles/2020/3/the-difference-between-emergency-remote-teaching-and-online-learning

Koehler, M. J., & Mishra, P. (2009). What is technological pedagogical content knowledge? *Contemporary Issues in Technology and Teacher Education, 9*(1), 60-70.

Quality Matters®. (2016). Quality Matters® Rubric. Maryland Online. Retrieved from https://www.quali- tymatters.org/grades-6-12-rubric

Reeves, M., Haanaes, K., & Sinha, J. (2015, June 24). Navigating the dozens of different strategy options. Harvard Business Review [Blog post]. Retrieved from https://hbr.org/2015/06/navigating-the-dozens-of-different-strategy-options

Ward, C. (2011, November). *The development of technological pedagogical content knowledge (TPACK) in instructors using Quality Matters training, rubric, and peer collaboration.* Presented at the 3rd Annual Quality Matters Conference, Baltimore, MD.

Human and Artificial Intelligence for the Society of the Future
Short Paper Book of the European Distance and E-Learning Network (EDEN)
2020 Annual Conference | Timisoara, 22-24 June, 2020
ISBN 978-615-5511-28-8

COMBINING PERSONALIZATION AND AUGMENTED REALITY IN A UNIVERSITY MUSEUM COLLECTION: THE INCLUSIVE MEMORY MOBILE APP

Antonella Poce, Francesca Amenduni, Marika Mascitti, Roma Tre University, Department of Educational Sciences, Italy

Abstract

University museums are powerful resource centres in higher education. In this context, the adoption of digital technologies can support personalized learning experience within university museum. Providing users' personalized learning paths could be crucial especially in the context of museum accessibility and social inclusion. For this purpose, our research group in the context of the Inclusive Memory project, founded by the University of Roma Tre, decided to develop the Inclusive Memory (IM) Mobile App aimed at detecting museum visitors profiles that can be used to provide inclusive learning paths for museum visitors'. The (IM) Mobile App also provides visitors the possibility to interact with the paintings through an Augmented Reality (AR) system. The IM Mobile App was tested in two pilot experimentation with a total of 29 university students. Data were collected and analysed by a combination of qualitative and quantitative methods. Some correlation among users' preferences, personal traits and fruition styles within the exhibition were detected. Students appreciated the exhibition, especially its multimodality. Most of the frequent themes identified in open-ended answers are related to Critical and Visual Thinking. Despite the positive overall evaluation, there is still room for improvement, both in terms of technology and educational design.

Introduction

University museums are powerful resource centres in higher education to enhance the impact of their teaching and research (Kelly, 2001). University museums provide unique opportunities to actively fulfil critical mission statements of university, by inspiring innovative research projects and providing students with real life objects to explore and manipulate (Boylan, 1999). Museum collections within the university setting offer a valuable opportunity to provide subject specific knowledge in various domains, from STEM education to arts and humanities. Museum objects can also be used to inspire discussion, group work and critical thinking – all crucial and transferable key skills in higher education. Recent reports promoted by the University Museum and Collections

Committee (UMAC) highlighted the role of digital and emergent technologies to further develop the presentation of museum collections through digital media to an ever widening audience (ICOM Study Series, 2003). Indeed, the adoption of digital technologies to support a personalized learning experience within museum contexts is a prominent trend. Museums can provide additional information through mobile apps, improving curiosity and engagement towards exhibitions and collections. As QR codes and smartphone apps have become widely used in museums all over the world, some museums are starting to explore ways to enhance the visitor experience through more interactive and customized devices (Ding, 2017). Specifically, Augmented Reality (AR) has become an accessible tool for promoting the interaction with real-world objects and pieces of arts included in museum collections. Different studies have highlighted that adopting AR solutions in museum contexts can support the visitors' overall experience (Jung, tom Dieck, Lee, & Chung, 2016), their intention to come back to the museum, their purchase intention (He, Wu, & Li, 2018) and a critical understanding of challenging knowledge (Yoon, Anderson, Lin, & Elinich, 2017).

Mobile applications could be also adopted to provide personalized learning paths in order to enhance user experience, attract new visitors and fulfil special needs of different kinds of visitors (Gaeta, Gaeta & Ritrovato, 2009). Personalization is based on the idea that an application can be designed to understand the user's needs, to provide the most relevant and efficient learning path in terms of visitors' educational needs. Its efficacy relies greatly on the validity and reliability of data collected about the user profile. Visitors' profile can be also defined as *personas*, an aggregate of target users who share common personal characteristics (Miaskiewicz, & Kozar, 2011). By inferring users' educational needs, motivations, and personality digital applications could provide visitors an adapted learning scenario within the museum environment. In the field of cultural heritage and museum education there are two main approaches for building *personas*: (Roussou et al., 2013): the explicit and the implicit approach. While in the explicit approach the visitor is directly asked to answer different kinds of questions, in the implicit approach the profile is built through the study of visitors' behaviours in the museum. Examples of implicit approaches are visitors' pattern of movement in the museum and eye-tracking. (Antoniou & Lepouras, 2010). Providing users' personalized learning paths could be crucial in the context of museum accessibility and social inclusion (Karimi, Zhang, & Benner, 2014). For this purpose, our research group in the context of the Inclusive Memory project decided to develop the Inclusive Memory (IM) Mobile App aimed at detecting museum visitors' profiles that can be used to provide inclusive learning paths enhanced by AR technologies and QR codes.

In the present work we will describe the results of two pilot experiences carried out within the Tito Rossini university painting collection, based at the Department of Education of the University of Roma Tre.

The context of the research and the research questions

The Tito Rossini's permanent exhibition is located at the Department of Education University Roma TRE, in the centre of Rome. The Centre for Museum Studies (CDM) of the Department of Education realized innovative mediation tools aimed at supporting visitors learning experience within the exhibition. Master degree students co-designed together with the teachers and CDM researchers different kinds of mediation tools with the aim to provide customizable learning paths according to the user needs.

Thus, heterogeneous and multimodal mediation tools were integrated into the IM mobile app designed to allow multiple and individualized visits. For each one of the Rossini's paintings considered, it was produced:

- An objective description of the work of art, from an art history point of view;
- An audio description of the work of art linked to a QR code;
- A short story acted, recorded and stored in the QR code;
- A music track;
- An AR animation.

Through the mobile device camera, the IM mobile app can recognize a piece of art uploaded in the database. When the application recognizes the painting, a digital version of the work of art appears on the screen together with a virtual assistant who propose a question for the user. Users can provide answers to a multiple-choice question and they can try to find the correct answer as many times as they want. For each correct answer, users can also visualize a part of a final question which it was designed to stimulate the reflection on the *trait d'union* among the different works of art. In this context, technology is thought to be employed in order to stimulate Critical Thinking skills in participants (Poce et al., 2019a).

The research was aimed at answering the following questions:

- How participants assess the visiting experience at the Tito Rossini exhibition?
- Are there any correlation among users' preferences, personal traits and fruition styles within the exhibition?
- Does the exhibition stimulate participants Critical Thinking?

Methods

The two experimental activities held at the Department of Education-Roma Tre University, based on a multimodal use of the contemporary art permanent exhibition *Tito Rossini,* involved 29 students in total (Average age: 30.5; Female = 25; Male = 2; Gender not specified = 2). In both the experimentation, the time devoted to the experience was two hours in total. In the initial phase, a brief introduction on the artist's biographical notes and a focus on the themes developed within his works were presented. Tito Rossini's work was contextualized in the broader Italian art scene of the early '900, by referring to important predecessors that inspired the entire work of the artist from Formia: Morandi, Carrà, Trombadori, Oppi.

In the first experimentation, at the beginning of the lesson, participants (N = 15; Female = 13; Male = 2; Average age: 36) were required to fill in the first questionnaire through the mobile-app. After that, they had the opportunity to visit the Tito Rossini permanent exhibition for approximately 60 minutes. Participants were invited by the teacher to use QR code to access to the paintings' written and audio descriptions, short stories and music tracks. After the visit, participants filled in the second questionnaires in which they are invited to express their preference on paintings and mediation tools. Participants' answers were automatically recorded by the web-app and converted in an excel-sheet. To guarantee participants' privacy, the data were collected anonymously and the pre and post-questionnaire were matched through a code.

In the second experimentation, at the end of the visit, students (N = 14; Average age: 25; Female = 12; Gender not specified = 2) were asked to fill in a questionnaire created through Google modules. The questionnaire was filled in anonymously in order to respect the participants' privacy and to not inhibit participants to also providing negative feedback regarding the exhibition. The questionnaire was made out of three sections:

- personal questions: gender, age and occupation (closed questions);
- Students' previous knowledge about the Tito Rossini exhibition, the evaluation of their learning experience, and suggestions for improving the learning path (both closed and open-ended questions).

Different kind of analysis were applied to the data. Average scores were calculated on quantitative data collected through closed-ended questions. In addition, correlations among users' preferences in terms of art, literature and mediation tools were calculated by using the software SPSS.

A theme analysis was applied to the open-ended-questions. Theme analysis is related to the classification of the patterns presented from qualitative data into themes. Through this technique, it is possible to bring together components or fragments of ideas or experiences, which often are meaningless when taken alone (1995). The aim of the thematic analysis was recognized if participants mentioned spontaneously themes related to Critical Thinking.

Results

From the total of 29 participants, 20 students had never heard about the artist Tito Rossini, 8 knew something about him and only one declared to know the artist very well. In addition, 13 students had noticed the exhibition in the University building before the visit, whilst 16 had never noticed the exhibition before. The following preliminary results show that the exhibition is not enough exploited and promoted at Departmental Level.

In the first experimentation, participants reported a general interest for the exhibition (Figure 1). Multimodality is generally appreciated. Short stories and music tracks did not receive a high average score (less than 2.5 out of 5) and this suggest there are still rooms for improvements.

After the visit, most of the participants reported curiosity towards the painting collection (53%). On the other hand, the 20% of the participants were bored during the exhibition and some of them felt restlessness. The 53.3% would suggest to visit the exhibition to other people, whilst the rest would not.

We detected a tendency between higher extroversion and preference for realistic art. For instance, ten out of fifteen participants who prefer a realistic painting was quite or very extroverted. On the other hand, lower extroversion seems to be more related with a romantic art preference and contemporary art.

Two people with higher extroversion level tend to prefer to visit the exhibition without the support of multimedia technologies, such as audio descriptions of the painting, short stories and music tracks. On the other hand, people with lower level of extroversion seem to prefer multimodality. More specifically, they appreciate combining the fruition of the painting while they listen the narration produced for that painting and soundtrack. Human guide is tendentially preferred by people with moderated level of extroversion.

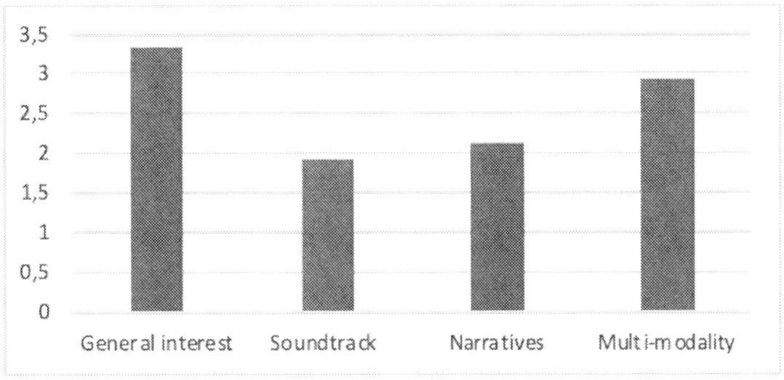

Figure 1. Level of satisfaction reported by visitors. Participants were required to express their level of satisfaction on a Likert scale (from 1 – *not satisfied* to 5 – *completely satisfied*)

In the second experimentation, participants were asked to assess their level of agreement with two negative statements and eight positive statements regarding the exhibition on a Likert scale from 1 (totally disagree) to 5 (totally agree). It is possible to see that the average scores for the two negative statements is lower than 3 (Figure 2). Thus, in average, participants did not prefer the traditional visit (Average = 2.78) compared to the multi-modal exhibition, and AR was not a distraction for them (Average = 2.86). On the other hand, regarding positive statements the average score was always higher than 3.5 which indicates a positive attitude towards different aspects of the exhibition. In particular, the highest average score was obtained for the statements "Multi-modality improves visitors' experience" (Average = 4.14) and the "The visit supported socialization with my peers" (Average = 4). Despite the general appreciation, the average is lower for the statements "I had fun during the visit" (Average = 3.57) and "Augmented reality supported in-depth observation of paintings" (Average = 3.5). These results suggest some room for improvement of the next experimentation.

From the theme analysis, the following topics emerged: *inquisitiveness* (25.93%) and *synthesis* (7.41%), both connected to Critical Thinking skills and dispositions. *Art* (14.81%), *visualization* (16,679) and *innovation* (1.85%) more connected to the definition of Visual thinking.

Other topics, which emerged from participants answers, are *technology* (18.52%), *collaboration* (5.56%), *travel* (5.56%), and *struggling* (3.7%). The topic of *travel* was associated with the topic of *art* through a meaningful metaphor used by one of the participant: "The exhibition was a journey through painted window".

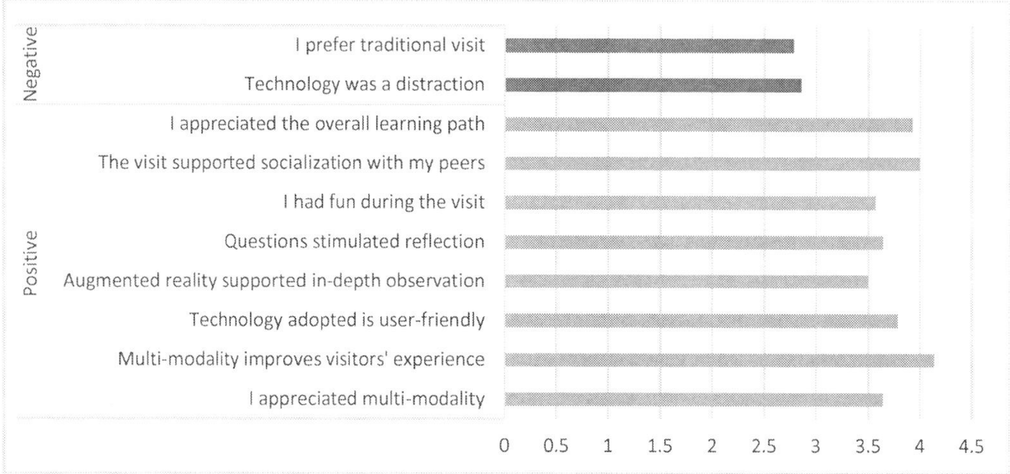

Figure 2. Participants' level of agreement with positive and negative statements regarding the exhibition. The level of agreement was expressed on a Likert Scale from 1 – *totally disagree* to 5 – *totally agree*

In figure 3 the positive and negative aspects of the Tito Rossini's exhibition according to participants are presented. The most appreciated features of the exhibition were the opportunity to identify a *Fil Rouge* among the paintings and to be stimulated by questions designed to support reflection. *Technology* was considered in both positive and critical aspects. Participants would also like to have the time to focus also on the other paintings and they did not always appreciate the arrangement of the paintings in the building.

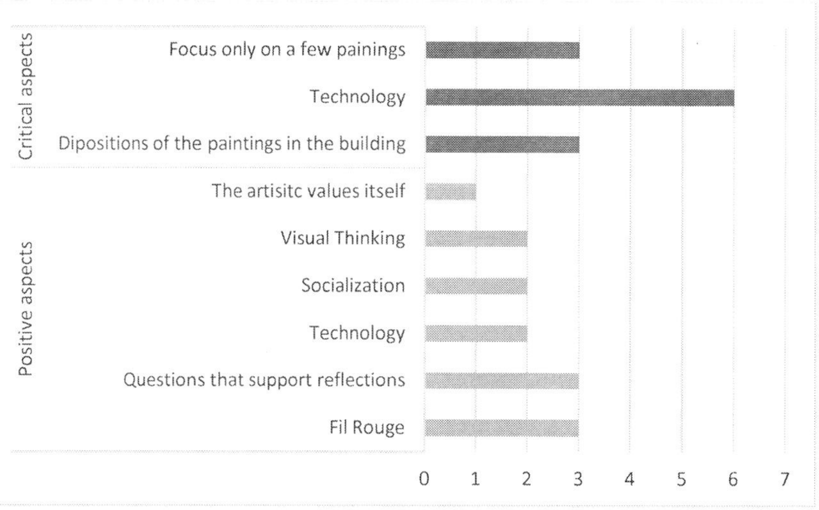

Figure 3. Positive and negative aspects of the exhibition according to the participants

Discussion and conclusive remarks

University museums provide unique opportunities to actively fulfil critical mission statements of higher education institutions (Boylan, 1999). Thus, it is necessary to think about efficient strategies to exploit University cultural heritage resources. Research has highlighted the role of digital technologies to improve users' experience within the museum context by providing personalized learning paths in order to enhance user experience, attract new visitors and fulfil special needs of different kinds of visitors. In this pilot research, we tested the IM mobile app developed to detect museum users' profiles in order to provide them personalized and accessible learning paths in the context of a university collection.

Most of the participants did not know about the exhibition neither the artist before the visit. This means that the Department of Education at Roma Tre University should find efficient solutions to better exploit its cultural heritage resources.

In the first experimentation, most of the participants reported curiosity towards the exhibition but a significant percentage reported feeling of boring and restlessness. More than half of the participants would suggest visiting the exhibition to other people, whilst the rest would not. These results encouraged us to re-design the visit, by enhancing the user experience with an AR application, tested in the second experimentation. Despite the number of participants does not allow any generalization, relations among artistic preference, personal traits and fruition modality was detected. From our perspective, the methodology here presented has the potential to improve the quality of learning path personalization in the context of the museum (Poce et al., 2019b).

In the second experimentation, most of the comments registered were positive. The exhibition seemed to have an impact on students' Critical Thinking enhancement because participants often reported topics related to thinking processes such as *inquisitiveness* and *analysis*. In addition, two of the most appreciated features of the exhibition were the opportunity to identify a *Fil Rouge* among the paintings and to be stimulated by questions designed to support critical reflection. For the next experimentation in the program, we will try to combine previously realized techniques with digital storytelling methodology, inserting stories and interactive music within the experience and giving users the chance to participate in the project by creating their digital content.

References

Antoniou, A., & Lepouras, G. (2010). Modeling visitors' profiles: A study to investigate adaptation aspects for museum learning technologies. *Journal on Computing and Cultural Heritage (JOCCH), 3*(2), 7.

Aronson, J. (1995). A pragmatic view of thematic analysis. *The qualitative report, 2*(1), 1-3.

Boylan, P. J. (1999). Universities and museums: Past, present and future. *Museum management and curatorship, 18*(1), 43-56.

Ding, M. (2017). Augmented reality in museums. Museums & augmented reality–A collection of essays from the arts management and technology laboratory, 1-15.

Gaeta, A., Gaeta, M., & Ritrovato, P. (2009). A grid based software architecture for delivery of adaptive and personalised learning experiences. *Personal and Ubiquitous Computing, 13*(3), 207-217.

He, Z., Wu, L., & Li, X. R. (2018). When art meets tech: the role of augmented reality in enhancing museum experiences and purchase intentions. *Tourism Management, 68*, 127-139.

ICOM Study Series. (2003) University Museums and Collections (edited by UMAC). vol.11. ISSN: 1020-5543

Jung, T., tom Dieck, M. C., Lee, H., & Chung, N. (2016). Effects of virtual reality and augmented reality on visitor experiences in museum. In Information and communication technologies in tourism 2016 (pp. 621-635). Springer, Cham.

Karimi, H. A., Zhang, L., & Benner, J. G. (2014). Personalized accessibility map (PAM): A novel assisted wayfinding approach for people with disabilities. *Annals of GIS, 20*(2), 99-108.

Kelly, M. (2001). *Managing University Museums. Education and Skills.* Organisation for Economic Cooperation and Development, Paris.

Miaskiewicz, T., & Kozar, K. A. (2011). Personas and user-centered design: How can personas benefit product design processes? *Design studies, 32*(5), 417-430.

Poce, A., Amenduni, F., De Medio, C., Valente, M., & Re, M. R. (2019a). Adopting Augmented Reality to Engage Higher Education Students in a Museum University Collection: the Experience at Roma Tre University. *Information, 10*(12), 373.

Poce, A., Re, M. R., Amenduni, F., De Medio, C., & Valente, M. (2019b). Developing a web App to provide personalized feedback for museum visitors: a pilot research project. *Form@ re-Open Journal per la formazione in rete, 19*(3), 48-59.

Roussou, M., Katifori, A., Pujol, L., Vayanou, M., & Rennick-Egglestone, S. J. (2013, April). A life of their own: museum visitor personas penetrating the design lifecycle of a mobile experience. In CHI'13 Extended Abstracts on Human Factors in Computing Systems (pp. 547-552). ACM.

Yoon, S., Anderson, E., Lin, J., & Elinich, K. (2017). How augmented reality enables conceptual understanding of challenging science content. *Journal of Educational Technology & Society, 20*(1), 156.

About the Authors

A. Poce coordinated the research presented in this paper. Research group is composed by the authors of the contribution that was edited in the following order: A. Poce (Introduction, Discussion and Conclusive Remarks) F. Amenduni (The context of the research and the research questions; Methods) M. Mascitti (Results).

Human and Artificial Intelligence for the Society of the Future
Short Paper Book of the European Distance and E-Learning Network (EDEN)
2020 Annual Conference | Timisoara, 22-24 June, 2020
ISBN 978-615-5511-28-8

STUDENTS' PERSPECTIVES ON STUDYING ONLINE IN TIMES OF COVID19 LEARNINGS FROM PODCAST CONVERSATIONS

Ulf-Daniel Ehlers, Laura Eigbrecht, Baden-Württemberg Cooperative State University Karlsruhe, Germany

Abstract

Higher education institutions are searching for strategies on how to face recent challenges and how to prepare students for an uncertain future, equipping them with the necessary skills. The Corona shutdown, with closed university buildings and a forced prompt digitization of higher education classes, has challenged them to quickly adapt to the new situation, trying out new ways of teaching and learning. A recently aired podcasting project is presenting the students' voices and their perceptions of their individual study experiences in times of the Corona shutdown – as well as their ideas for future higher education. First results show demands to the institutions in learning about digital and interactive teaching as well as a tendency to foster self-organizational skills on an individual level.

Introduction

The month of March 2020 has been a significant one for most people: the measures taken by governments – be it regional, national or supranational (such as the European Union) – have changed almost everybody's everyday lives. This also holds true for students: Higher Education is at a turning point, where the classical model of lectures and seminars in lecture halls and classrooms can no longer be performed. While digitization has been a crucial strategic subject for higher education for years, the progress and changes performed in institutions of higher education differ greatly. There is now a point where instant digitization is demanded in order to find solutions for making studying possible for students and for providing them with ongoing quality education. Some institutions are better prepared for this – others are less. However, they meet the same challenges of enabling students to pursue their studies from home or any place they might be at. The process of studying in times of the Corona Shutdown brings studying back to the very individual, more than ever: They are mostly in a situation where they have to organize their studies at home, sometimes all by themselves and with mostly digital interactions.

This has implications for learning processes, self-organization in terms of time and space, interactions with friends, lecturers and fellow students and also on a psychological level.

A possible outcome of this would be for higher education institutions to find new ways of engaging students in digital teaching formats, thus enhancing their learning experience and pursuing these learnings when attendance classes will be possible again. Another one would be for students to learn about themselves and to enhance their competences when it comes to self-organization – thus building *Future Skills* such as Learning Competence, Self-efficacy, Self-competence and Initiative & Performance Competence, competences or *Future Skills* closely related to the individual development (Ehlers, 2020). When approaching those questions, it is important to take into account the views of the students themselves.

Almost 20 years ago we have established a learner's quality paradigm for digital learning (Ehlers, 2003). Today, in these challenging times, leading the global world of higher education to undergo a big digital and educational change process, we would like to come back to this idea. Therefore, we have set up a podcast series in which we broadcast students' voices. The podcast intends to interview students about their experiences in times of the Covid 19 or Corona Shutdown. The podcast "Studium im Shutdown" ("Studying during Shutdown") is taking the students' perspective, asking them about how studying functions for them at home, what strategies they are developing as well as about their demands and wishes for higher education institutions. The podcast gives insights into students' ways of coping with the recent situation – for other students who can relate, but also for higher education professionals, learning about possible ways for a successful future higher education. The interviews can be seen as qualitative material on the subject of self-organization and digital learning in order to draw conclusions on those matters for the strategic development of higher education. The project can be understood within the larger framework of student-centred higher education and designing participation-oriented higher education contexts. This also constitutes the link to our recent study on *Future Skills*, which shows the enormous demand for higher education designs which allow for the development of self-organization skills and competences instead of pre-defined knowledge transfer (Ehlers, 2020; Ehlers & Kellermann, 2019).

This paper provides insight into the first findings. We will describe the research methodology (section 2), give an insight into the first findings (section 3), reflect on podcasting as a qualitative research method (section 4) and give a summary and outlook (section 5) on how we will proceed with the project.

Research methodology: Obtaining qualitative data through podcasting

The project is a broadcasting and research one at the same time. Research design and journalistic reflections thus go hand in hand. Things that matter for a researcher – comparability of different interview materials, for example – might not be as interesting to the listener or audience. We thus have a qualitative research set with half-structured interviews – an interview guide with pre-set questions and keywords serving as a basis for the conversations – serving as raw material for the podcasts which, then, will be edited to a selective format with quotations expected to be interesting to the audience. However, due to the different profiles of the interviewees, some singular questions may not be asked or answered, others may be added. The raw interview material can thus serve – but with limitations – as a basis for qualitative content analysis (Mayring, 2015). We can analyse the interview material and find different answering categories in the individual and subjective stories.

By collecting individual narratives, we can find indications on personal study strategies, self-organization skills on self-study competencies. We can also collect data on higher education institutions' approaches to creating a virtual classroom feeling, of fostering interactivity and the interviewees' perceptions of how well these approaches are put into action and working. We can thus draw very first conclusions on digital study strategies both on the side of institutions and students and learn about how well they may function in the future.

The first episode of the Podcast "Studium im Shutdown" aired on April 6, 2020 followed by two new weekly episodes average. Up until now (27th of May 2020), thirteen episodes have been released, each between six and ten minutes long. The interviews have been conducted and released in German and with students studying and living in Germany. A broader perspective is being prepared, interviewing students in different European countries about their study experiences. The podcast is being recorded at distance via ZOOM, edited on Audacity and disseminated via a special Website dedicated to the format but also via Anchor FM and RSS feed to platforms such as Spotify (this being the most frequented with 44% of all listeners), Apple Podcast, Deezer, Google Podcast (Source: Anchor FM).

Recruitment has happened via personal contacts, but also externally with students learning about the project and contacting the team via email. Students interviewed so far are studying in different disciplines (Business Studies, Business Informatics, Medicine, European history and culture, Music, Psychology, International Relations, Teacher Training, Physics, Law, Media Management, Applied Health Studies) and at different higher education institutional forms ('classic' university, University of Applied Sciences, Technical University, Dual Studies, PhD programme). A diversity in disciplines and study environment is intended. Students interviewed are living alone, sharing a house with their families or living in shared flats.

The podcast format is structured into five parts, introduced and closed by a jingle and separated by short bumpers. The first one is a short introduction to the podcast subject by the presenter, who is a member of the research team. Then follows a part on what the interviewed person's study subject is and how studies usually take place. Then we ask about the ways in which studies take place nowadays in times of the Corona shutdown. We then ask about personal strategies to cope with the situation – both with staying focussed but also for personal well-being and conclude with the question on what higher education institutions should learn from this for the future.

The collected data are reviewed by the research team of four persons, and regular reports summarising the issues raised by the students are established.

Description of the first findings

In total 13 qualitative interviews have taken place so far which equal a total length of 466 minutes or almost eight hours of audio-recorded interview material. For the edited podcasts, a short introduction by the presenter is combined with some recorded questions, but mostly with the interviewee's recordings, those being edited according to criteria such as reflectiveness, originality and being relatable. The presenter's part of asking questions and commenting on answers is only left in the edited podcast when necessary for understanding the interviewee's answers – their perceptions being the central concern of the podcast. The different main themes of the podcast – structured into five parts and respective sub-questions – serve as a scheme for analysing the material, the answers being clustered and compared within the thematic categories, thus allowing first insights into the range of students' recent realities and perceptions of their study situation. Some first observations shall be presented here. Considering the small scope of the project so far, more elaborate and valid results can be expected, perspectively taking international perspectives into account.

First analyses show that the audience numbers have steadily risen from the beginning, with press reports and social media coverage equally doing so. Most listeners come from Germany, some from France and very few from Sweden, Ireland and Italy. In Germany, most listeners are located in North Rhine-Westphalia, Baden-Württemberg (where our institution is located) and Lower Saxony. Most listeners are female with 63%, followed by male with 31% and each 3% not specified and Non-binary (Source: Spotify). Most listeners are in the age of "classic" students (66% aged 18-27, 30% from 18-22 and 36% from 23-27) according to Spotify. The third group with a percentage of 12% is that of people aged 28-34, followed by 45-59 with 9% (note the different category sizes). However, since Spotify statistics cover only a very selective range of the podcast listeners, these indications are only rough ones.

General Observations

All students approached were happy to participate and took great enthusiasm in the project. Some thanked the team and were happy to "finally be able to do something". The concept of giving an active voice to students thus seems to function, the podcast serving as a medium to overcome a personally perceived passivity. We are further developing this idea to see how podcasting can serve to reinforce and support student-centred learning methodology as well as participatory approaches to higher education.

Observations on the "normal times" before COVID19

Most students interviewed indicated that not many courses have incorporated digital teaching methods so far – this being a common element across higher education institutions. If at all, this was then done through audience response systems' usage during class or digital platforms such as Moodle for distributing materials. All of them wished for more digital elements, especially for allowing more flexible ways of studying.

Online learning in COVID19 times

The respondents are indicating that there are different levels of how classes are being digitized: by pure uploading of lecture scripts, by synchronous live lectures and by asynchronous classes, with chat modules, video conferences and interactive parts. The providing of bare study materials without any ways of interacting was mostly negatively perceived, one student even acting on this and asking for more input from the lecturer's side. There seems to be a preference to interactive forms of studying – these presenting a way of normality perceived as helpful, but there also is a certain understanding for the special situation on the institutional side: Students seem to be very understanding on digital lectures not being "perfect" yet, as long as communication from the institutional side is clear and transparent. This benignity is dropping the more subjects such as examinations and graduating become prominent in the individual study situation. All in all, students ask for interaction and active learning – pure knowledge acquisition seems too little; they ask for ways of debating, applying and exchanging, thus enhancing competencies based on knowledge. Students interviewed are active learners that want to understand and not only pass examinations. They also want to be individually perceived and visible with their individual issues and questions. Students also observed a positive evolution amongst teachers: those being sceptical towards digital teaching now having mastered the tools have now partly taken a more positive view concerning this matter. However, several interviewees expressed the perception that their workload is much higher right now than usually, due to having to learn about new tools but mostly to many more individual and highly paced tasks to hand in.

Personal learning and study strategies

Interviewed students have developed a wide range of self-organized ways of learning and living. There is a co-working space set up within a shared flat, thus raising interdisciplinary discourses, there is a personal gym being set up in a family home, there is a music student jamming with a virtual band on YouTube and a student changing study spots throughout the day in order to imitate moving across campus. Virtual tools such as videoconferencing and messengers are important to keep in touch with friends, but also very distracting and menacing concentration capacities. The need for structure is high, most students thus determining certain areas of their personal space for work and others for leisure activities, with self-scheduled breaks for walks and sports. They appreciate clearly scheduled classes with clear time frames being set up. Some have developed new hobbies, such as sewing, writing poems. A lot of students take new interest in tidying up, redecorating their homes. There is a shared anticipation for when "things will be normal again" with a certain insecurity on when this will be the case again. Most students interviewed showed a high level of reflection, reflecting on learning about themselves, on what it means to be thrown back to oneself and what can be kept from this for the future. Most students seemed to have developed various and successful ways of coping; none of those interviewed were in a threatening situation such as having lost an important job etc., suffering from loneliness and anxieties. It is also possible that those private concerns were perceived as too intimate to share them in a podcast. A shared issue, however, was that it is important to "keep oneself busy" in order to cope with the recent situation.

Expectations on Future Higher Education

There seems to be a consensus among students that higher education institutions must learn from this and cannot go back to "normal" when attendance classes will be allowed again. Students wish for more digital teaching formats for allowing more flexibility, inclusion and expect institutions to be more open towards change, interdisciplinarity and subjects such as sustainability. They ask for more options of how to approach certain study contents.

Reflections on potential and limitations of podcasting as a qualitative research method

Podcast interviews are a special methodological context of interviewing. The qualitative data which can be obtained through the recorded conversations during a podcast interview are a side effect of the podcast production itself. We have written about using online and digital media for data – especially qualitative – before (Ehlers 2005). Back then, podcasting was still at its very beginning. Today, podcasting proves to be a useful and specific form of qualitative interviewing. It can be understood as a semi-structured form of an online interview, and it is thematically focussed. Our special format is up-front designed to focus on extracting certain short limited sequences of the topic in question – both interviewer and interviewee know this. In addition to that and as we have learned in our case, the students which we interviewed also took on a perspective of representing the students as a whole and not just talking about their own personal viewpoints. This was partly motivated through the way we asked (e.g. "What can universities do better?") but also because they know already during the interview situation that the material will be potentially broadcast. This way, a special interview atmosphere is created.

For podcasting interviews, the same principles apply as to qualitative research – be it online or not: openness in the research situation and towards the researched person and explication of the presuppositions. However, there are some additional aspects to be considered. It can be noticed that podcast interviews provide a changed contextuality: a limited possibility of establishing a personal, empathic relationship between the researcher and the researched which leads to a fundamentally changed nature of the research situation and thus also of the data generated here. However, it is explicitly emphasized that contextuality as a characteristic cannot be less or more present, but rather represents a constitutive element of any survey situation. Only the nature of contextuality can be present in different forms or can be deduced in different ways.

For the qualitative interpretation process it is necessary to include the contextuality of the respective data collection situation, since subjective structures of meaning always manifest themselves in concrete contexts. In online-supported data collection procedures, contextual information – for example, about the concrete survey situation of the researcher – can only be obtained by verbal explication due to the spatial separation of researcher and researched. A special feature of the podcasting interview is its narrative nature due to which often additional context information are given by the interviewed. One advantage of podcasting and interviewing online is the (mostly) automatic data recording. When using online media, generated data is automatically logged. This is done either in a simple way as a simple text document – for example a chat session – or as a complete interaction recording via video of the data collection process in collaboration environments. In our case, it is done by an audio recording.

A necessary criterion for success – and thus also a barrier to participation – for online-supported data collection processes is a pronounced media usage competence of all participants. Especially for qualitative data collection, it is necessary that researchers and researched persons are able to handle the existing communication possibilities perfectly in a communication situation that is limited to text or image exchange. A peculiarity at the beginning of online-supported – especially synchronous – data collection processes is therefore a great self-referentiality of the contributions with regard to the situation. Participants often refer to their own, and for them at first unfamiliar, communication situation by trying out the technical possibilities offered or communicating via these. It is therefore advisable to place a short introductory sequence at the beginning of each online-supported survey situation.

A further characteristic of successful generation of qualitative data through podcasting is the dependence of the survey situation on the personal relation of the participants. If the participants know each other personally well, narrative and discussion elements are more readily apparent and provide more productive data material. For this reason, moderators in virtual group discussions often organize so-called ice-breaking activities (virtual champagne reception, introduction rounds) at the beginning of a podcasting sequence. Here it is important that each participant gets a longer speech or writing part to get used to the special communication situation and to become familiar with the medium. The presenter in our project usually takes a few minutes in the beginning to get to know the interviewee and explain how the interview will take place and how we will proceed afterwards.

Summary and outlook

First results indicate that higher education institutions can learn from this situation on how to implement digital teaching in order to enhance students' study experiences, those asking for more interactivity, inclusion and flexibility. There is strong evidence that students develop diverse coping mechanisms and thus strengthen their self-organization capacities related to the fostering of different *Future Skills*. However, these are only first results and very individual stories in semi-structured interview sessions. The students interviewed are not representative; this being a podcasting project and thus being more of an explorative study. However, more podcasts will be produced and provide insights into students' perceptions of digital teaching and individual ways of learning, but also of virtual presence. The range of disciplines will be extended; international perspectives will also be heard. It must be noted that progress and change is fast these days and teaching might change on a daily basis – lecturers also learning about new teaching methods and incorporating them more and more – this already becoming evident in 'later' podcasts. Thus, the interviews can be set in contrast to each other and must each be interpreted in the individual students' situation at a certain time and space – institutions are adopting more and more to the not-so-new situation. It is important to listen to students' voices in this process and to take the chance to learn from them about which ways of digital teaching work for them and which don't – and about what they expect from their institutions in the future.

References

Ehlers, U.-D. (2003). *Qualität beim E-Learning. Empirische Grundlegung und Modellkonzeption einer subjektorientierten Qualitätsentwicklung.* Bielefeld: Unpublished dissertation.

Ehlers, U.-D. (2005). Qualitative Onlinebefragung. In L. Mikos, & C. Wegener (Eds.), *Handbuch Qualitative Medienforschung* (pp 279-290). Stuttgart: UVK/UTB.

Ehlers, U.-D. (2020). *Future Skills – Future Learning and Future Higher Education.* Wiesbaden: Springer.

Ehlers, U.-D., & Kellermann, S. A. (2019). *Future Skills. The Future of Learning and Higher education. Results of the International Future Skills Delphi Survey.* Karlsruhe. Retrieved from https://nextskills.org/future-skills-report-2019

Mayring (2015). *Qualitative Inhaltsanalyse: Grundlagen und Techniken.* Weinheim & Basel: Beltz.

Mikos, L., & Wegener, C. (Eds.) (2005). *Handbuch Qualitative Medienforschung.* Stuttgart: UVK/UTB.

Podcast Domains

https://studium-im-shutdown.de/

https://anchor.fm/studium-im-shutdown

ISBN 978-615-5511-28-8

ECCOE

European Credit Clearinghouse for Opening up Education

Website: http://eccoe.eu

Runtime: 09.2019 – 08.2022

Supported / co-funded by: Erasmus+ KA2 Strategic Partnerships

Partners: Fondation-UNIT-AUNEGe (FR) – coordinator; Knowledge Innovation Centre (MT); UNED (ES); Politecnico di Milano – METID (IT); Vytautas Magnus University (LT); EADTU (NL).

Project representative to be contacted for further info: Deborah Arnold (deborah.arnold@aunege.fr)

Short description of the initiative:

ECCOE, the European Credit Clearinghouse for Opening up Education, aims to facilitate the endorsement and appropriation of open, online and flexible higher education by increasing trust in technology-enabled credentials among students, higher education institutions (HEIs) and employers. To this end, the project is developing a complete solution in the form of an ECCOE-system, with publicly-reviewed credential descriptors, Model Credit Recognition Agreements, an online catalogue of over 60 disciplinary and transversal modules, a robust solution for technology-enabled credentials and a network of stakeholder users.

Main target groups of the project: Higher Education Institutions: academic staff (programme directors, teachers and faculty deans) and professional staff (international, legal departments, student administration units); learners; employers.

Significant public results:

By the time of the EDEN2020 Annual Conference, the first public results will be ready for the launch of the first rounds of public consultation and open peer review.

Model Credit Recognition Agreement: open peer review June-Nov 2020

Online catalogue of disciplinary and transversal modules: first collection June-Dec 2020

Quality criteria for the description of credentials: launch of first public consultation Oct 2020

Technology-enabled credentials: public consultation on improved metadata standards Oct 2020-Jan 2021

Abstract

ECCOE, the European Credit Clearinghouse for Opening up Education, supports the drive towards more open, online and flexible higher education. Policy makers at European and national level are responding to the needs of an increasingly diversified student population with calls for a more modular approach to credentials, and employers are focusing more and more on the actual competences that graduates are able to demonstrate. Furthermore, in the current political climate, transnational mobility, whether physical, virtual or a combination of the two, is a powerful vehicle for increasing cross-cultural awareness.

For this vision to become reality, there is a great need for a solid, trustworthy system supporting cross-institution recognition of credits at the level of courses or modules. Over and above the technology, such recognition will not take off without appropriate quality mechanisms and the demonstration that the overall process, the ECCOE-system, has been tried and tested with a critical mass of stakeholders.

The main goal of ECCOE is thus to facilitate the endorsement and appropriation of open, online and flexible higher education. In support of this overarching objective, the project aims to increase trust in technology-enabled credentials among students, higher education institutions (HEIs) and employers. In support of sustainable take-up, ECCOE is committed to the use of open meta data based on ESCO (European Skills, Competences, Qualifications and Occupations), open source codes and Creative Commons licences.

The benefits for HEIs include greater efficiency, quality and transparency for lifelong learning. Students will benefit from flexible opportunities in support of transnational mobility as well as improvements in employability, being able to demonstrate competency-based credentials both for degree-level qualifications and for recognition by employers. In terms of societal impact, the trust-based ECCOE-system will open up opportunities for citizens to develop intercultural skills through flexible, transnational lifelong learning.

ISBN 978-615-5511-28-8

eLene4Life

Learning and Interacting to Foster Employability

Website: http://elene4life.eu/

Runtime: 09.2018 – 08.2021

Supported / co-funded by: Erasmus+ KA2 Grant Agreement N°: 2018-1-FR01-KA203-047829

Partners: Fondation UNIT – AUNEGe (FR) (Coordinator), Fondazione Politecnico di Milano (IT), Politecnico di Milano (IT), European University College Association (BE), Warsaw University of Technology (PL), Universität Bremen (DE), Liberia Universita Maria SS Assunta di Roma (IT), University of Dundee (UK)

Project representative to be contacted for further info: Deborah Arnold (deborah.arnold@aunege.fr)

Short description of the initiative:

eLene4Life supports curriculum innovation in higher education (HE) through the development of active learning approaches for soft skills, with the ultimate aim of improving students' employability. The main aims of eLene4Life are to:

- overcome skills mismatches with respect to transversal skills;
- develop new innovative curricula and educational methods integrating active learning, at the same time addressing commonly encountered barriers such as large class sizes and physical spaces.
- improve the relevance of HE curricula in Partner Countries in a VUCA (Volatile, Uncertain, Complex, Ambiguous) world.

To achieve these goals, eLene4Life has conducted transnational analysis of active learning for soft skills in HE and the corporate sector, produced a Lessons Learned Kit drawing on these two analyses, and developed a Dynamic Toolkit describing 30 active learning methods which are currently being piloted in 5 countries. The next step is to build on the results of these pilots to develop a discussion-based MOOC for teacher professional development.

The driving idea behind eLene4Life is cross-fertilisation between the higher education and corporate sectors. This is supported by the eLene4Life trans-sectoral Community of Practice, through national Working Groups and a social media ecosystem.

Main target groups of the project: HE leaders, teachers, students, alumni; HR managers, trainers, training providers.

Significant public results:

- **Transnational analysis** on active learning methods for soft-skills development – HE report
- **Transnational analysis** on active learning methods for soft-skills development – corporate report
- **Lessons Learned Kit N°1**: active learning for soft skills in the HE and corporate sectors

These reports, and other resources, can be accessed via the eLene4Life website www.elene4life.eu or directly via the flashcode:

eLene4Life – Learning and Interacting to Foster Employability

The eLene4Life **Dynamic Toolkit**: a selection of 30 ready-to-use active learning methods for soft skills: http://elene4life.eu/dynamic-toolkit/

The eLene4Life **Community of Practice** is active across a variety of social media. You can contribute to the conversation, share your experience and be inspired by others through:

- joining the LinkedIn group Active Learning for Soft Skills Development (https://www.linkedin.com/groups/13778700/)
- joining the eLene Network group on Facebook (https://www.facebook.com/groups/eLenenetwork/)
- following the @eLene2learn account and #eLene4Life, #softskills #activelearning on Twitter
- writing a guest blog post on the eLene4Life hub (contact Deborah.Arnold@aunege.fr)

ISBN 978-615-5511-28-8

CoLED

Collaborative Learning Environment for Engineering Education

Website: http://coled-project.eu/

Runtime: 10.2018 – 09.2020

Supported / co-funded by: ERASMUS+

Partners: PIAP – Poland; PRO-MED – Poland; University of Medicine, Pharmacy, Science and Technology of Târgu Mureș – Romania; AidLearn, Consultoria em Recursos Humanos Lda. – Portugal; ECQ – Bulgaria

Project representative to be contacted for further info: Jacek Zieliński (jzielinski@piap.pl)

Main target groups of the project:

- Entrepreneurs and enterprise employees aiming to improve competitiveness of their parent companies and their own qualifications.
- Prospective entrepreneurs and students willing to develop manufacturing businesses.
- Universities and research centres.
- VET trainers and VET suppliers.

Significant public results:

- Teaching Methodology – a methodology including detailed information on actual needs requirements and preferences of target groups and guidelines for using CoLED platform and available teaching materials.
- Guides – a short description of portal functions and teaching materials.
- Training Platform – an innovative ICT platform supporting common teaching, group interactions, teaching gamification, group communication, evaluation of team tasks and projects, group discussions, identification of user activity etc.
- Training – practice-based teaching resources for anyone interested in introducing solutions for automation and robotics.

Abstract

Collaborative Learning Environment for engineering education (CoLED) is an European project implemented within the framework of Erasmus+ Programme, Key Action 2: Cooperation for innovation and the exchange of good practices. The CoLED consortium consist of 5 partners from 4 different European countries – Bulgaria, Poland, Portugal and Romania, all of which have extensive expertise and relevant experience in developing transnational projects. The project activities are scheduled to be implemented between October 2018 and September 2020.

According to recent research, deep learning and the development of critical and higher order thinking skills only occur through interaction and collaboration. Although collaborative learning is widely known and used in different learning approaches, the concept of collaborative learning supported by the modern ICT technologies for the vocational training for the methods of successful implementation of automation solutions in manufacturing is a factor which makes CoLED project approach innovative.

The general aim of CoLED project is to develop an innovative collaborative training approach including curricula and ICT training online collaboration learning solution in the field connected with introduction of automation for enterprises and other people interested in those areas. The CoLED project will focus on development of new dedicated ICT solutions integrated with eLearning platform supporting of collaboration learning, positive interdependence, individual accountability, face-to-face and online promotional interaction, appropriate use of collaborative skills, group processing.

Human and Artificial Intelligence for the Society of the Future
Short Paper Book of the European Distance and E-Learning Network (EDEN)
2020 Annual Conference | Timisoara, 22-24 June, 2020
ISBN 978-615-5511-28-8

RE-SERVES

REsearch at the SERVice of Educational fragilitieS

Website: http://www.dsu.univr.it/?ent=progetto&id=5450&lang=en

Runtime: 08/2019-08/2022

Supported / co-funded by: Ministero dell'Istruzione dell'Università e della Ricerca, PRIN2017

Partners: University of Verona, Italy; University of Sister Orsola Benincasa, Italy; University of Rome TRE, Italy; Kore University of Enna, Italy

Project representative to be contacted for further info: Francesco Agrusti (francesco.agrusti@uniroma3.it)

Short description of the initiative:

ARE-SERVES aims at deepening understandings of the relations between fragility, vulnerability and education, through analyses and problematisation of existing educational practices in a variety of contexts. Building on this knowledge RE-SERVEs aims also at proposing a hermeneutic horizon for designing new policies and practices. The relationships education holds to vulnerability (at both individual, and structural and societal levels) and frailty groups of people, communities of place, and identity are still underexplored, at least within the Italian context. Comprehending such relations, however, is a pre-requisite for ensuring inclusive and quality education for all and promoting lifelong learning in Italy.

Main target groups of the project: RE-SERVES will contribute to exploring these relations by focusing on four topical issues: (a) Civic disengagement: Contemporary sociological and philosophical analyses describe our society as characterized by indifference and individualism. (b) Adolescents' aggressive and violent behaviours: the spread of antisocial, aggressive, and violent behaviours amongst adolescents, often leads to deviant, delinquent, and criminal actions. (c) Youth social and economic exclusion: In Italy, according to 2013 Eurofound data, the proportion of people with physical problems among young not in employment, education or training (NEET) is lower (0.9%) than the European average (1.1%), this project intends to explore, analyse and evaluate the potentialities of employing MOOCs in support of NEETs' reengagement in learning, and in a type of learning that can help them in the search for jobs and to re-enter the about market. (d) The frailty of incoming migrants and unaccompanied minors: this project problematizes the non-formal educational practices, in particular those adopted by the second reception centres that have been called, since 2016, to design educational interventions and strategies aimed at guiding the unaccompanied foreign minors through a process of growth, and the development of personal and social identity, in order to foster their progressive responsibility and autonomy.

Abstract

RE-SERVES focuses attention on fragility and vulnerability issues in education, within the Italian context. Both fragility and vulnerability holds complex and multifaceted relations with education; accordingly, RE-SERVES builds on a composite research design. Besides its main focus on the relations between fragility, vulnerability and education, the project is structured in four sub-areas of in-depth investigation on topical issues in the Italian contemporary society, namely: civic dis-engagement; adolescents' aggressive and violent behaviours; youth social and economic exclusion; and the frailty of incoming migrants and unaccompanied minors. While assuming a collective form, the project builds on an organic and structured framework in regards to its epistemological, methodological, political and ethical instances, so as to avoid the risk of fragmentation. But to allow for in-depth investigations, each topical issue identified by the project is made the centre of attention by a research unit. Accordingly, the project is organized in six Work Packages (WPs), of which WPs 1-4 are research-specific, and WPs 5-6 are dedicated to project management and dissemination activities, respectively.

Human and Artificial Intelligence for the Society of the Future
Short Paper Book of the European Distance and E-Learning Network (EDEN)
2020 Annual Conference | Timisoara, 22-24 June, 2020
ISBN 978-615-5511-28-8

UFN

University of the Future Network

Website: https://unifuture.network

Runtime: April.20.2016 – Current

Supported / co-funded by: Caixa Bank, Hagen Universität, UPenn University, Milano Biccoca / UFN network

Partners: Open University of Catalunya, University of Alberta, see more at: https://unifuture.network

Project representative to be contacted for further info: Martha Burkle (burkle@ualberta.ca), Josep Duart (jduart@uoc.edu)

Short description of the initiative: The project of creating a network of academics, researchers and industry partners to examine and envision the future of universities (and their role in distance learning) started with the idea of responding to the challenges that universities around the world are facing with regard to student retention, funding allocation, research relevance. It was (and still is) important to consider how are universities responding to the expectations of the labour force, particularly at the industry level. Little we knew then about the huge challenges that COVID-19 was going to bring to the traditional university delivery of courses and credentials.

With funding from Caixa Bank, Catalonia, creators of the idea started by putting together a team of experts who came from all over the world: Europe, North and South America, and Africa. Their immediate goal was to work as a 'think-tank' in the identification of policies and strategies that could help universities as they develop strategic plans to continue to be relevant in the future panorama of universal education.

Main target groups of the project: academic institutions, doctoral students, industry partners

Significant public results: Annual meetings, research reports, meetings with PhD candidates, technology oriented industries presentations, policy analysis for online learning, research projects for technology applications, recommendation blue print documents for organizations converting online, etc.

Abstract

The University of the Future Network is a multidisciplinary and international consortium where researchers and academics meet to analyse and discuss the challenges and opportunities that universities are facing in the framework of the 21st century. It is a network that explores, discusses, envisions the future of universities, linking its work with doctoral candidates and with industry oriented start up and companies.

The construction of the international network emerges with the arrival of the new Millennium, as universities were subdue by: (a) financial restrictions, (b) radical changes in the students' education expectations (c) high demand from industry to get graduates with relevant work competencies.

UFN – University of the Future Network

UFN members want to be at the core of universities' transformation, developing research projects, learning from each other, building capacity among universities in developing countries which are facing similar challenges without the resources and capabilities of the industrialized world.

So far, the network has met four times in four different countries. Each meeting is presided by work done between the network founders and the hosting university, linking with local research projects and identifying potential doctoral students whose research work is linked to online education (in all its forms), or to the development of innovative curriculum, or to creating a technology oriented start company. Working with the network partners, higher education institutions have received guidance to develop new online programs, or feedback about linking the work of graduates to industry needs. Furthermore, members of the network have also great impact in local research institutions and/or government bodies, by bring innovative ideas that contribute to the creation of a more sustainable and inclusive society.

ISBN 978-615-5511-28-8

ENRICH in China

ENRICH – European Network of Research and Innovation Centres and Hubs, China (ERICENA project)

Website: www.china.enrichcentres.eu

Runtime: 01.2017 – 12.2020

Supported / co-funded by: European Commission's DG Research & Innovation

Partners: Sociedade Portuguesa de Inovação (SPI), Portugal, see more at: http://china.enrichcentres.eu/consortium

Project representative to be contacted for further info: Sara Medina (saramedina@spi.pt)

ERICENA stands for European Research and Innovation Centre of Excellence in ChiNA (ERICENA). It is a Horizon 2020 project selected for funding under the ENG-GLOBALLY-9-2016 call which aims to support European science, technology and innovation (STI) in China through the creation of a service-based centre. ERICENA was selected for funding together with two "sister projects", with similar goals for Brazil and the USA – these projects are named CEBRABIC and NearUS, respectively.

In order to more clearly distinct the projects from the centres intended to be created, the coordinators of ERICENA, CEBRABIC and NearUS, together with the European Commission (EC), decided to create a common brand for the centres, named as **ENRICH - European Network of Research and Innovation Centres and Hubs.**

ENRICH – European Network of Research and Innovation Centres and Hubs, China, offers unique services to European research, technology and business organisations, connecting them to the Chinese market. ENRICH in China aims to promote all the scientific and technology collaborative potential of the Chinese market for the benefit of European research organisations and technology based companies, including start-ups and SMEs. ENRICH in China has its headquarters in Beijing and a regional Hub in Chengdu, hosted by EUPIC.

ENRICH in China has 7 distinct service categories: RDI Consultancy and Coaching, STI RDI Intelligence, Soft Landing and Co-working, Fostering Open Innovation through Training, Cooperation Enabling Events, RDI Briefings and Innovation Support Certification. The service portfolio of ENRICH in China intends to be comprehensive and diverse, aiming at addressing the needs and interests of its European clients in the Chinese market and maximizing the benefits of their activities and presence in China.

Main target groups of the project: Research actors (universities, research centres), innovation actors (innovation and funding agencies, STI networks and platforms), business actors (large companies, SMEs, start-ups, clusters, business associations and chambers)

Significant public results:

- Events: http://www.china.enrichcentres.eu/events
- STI RDI Intelligence: http://www.china.enrichcentres.eu/reports

ENRICH in China – ENRICH – European Network of Research and Innovation Centres and Hubs, China (ERICENA project)

Abstract

ENRICH – European Network of Research and Innovation Centres and Hubs, China, offers unique services to European research, technology and business organisations, connecting them to the Chinese market. ENRICH in China has its headquarters in Beijing and a regional Hub in Chengdu, hosted by EUPIC. The service portfolio of ENRICH in China intends to be comprehensive and diverse, aiming at addressing the needs and interests of its European clients in the Chinese market and maximizing the benefits of their activities and presence in China. ENRICH in China aims to build a broad community across Europe and China, allowing for research, innovation and business actors to engage through different means and with different levels of involvement. In this sense, our community is built upon three main categories that are officially linked to the centre: Soft Landing Zones, External Service Providers, and Members. The objective of the training is to demonstrate how ENRICH in China is triggering all the scientific and technology collaborative potential of the Chinese market for the benefit of European research organisations and technology based companies including start-ups and SMEs.

Human and Artificial Intelligence for the Society of the Future
Short Paper Book of the European Distance and E-Learning Network (EDEN)
2020 Annual Conference | Timisoara, 22-24 June, 2020
ISBN 978-615-5511-28-8

NEXUS

Promoting the nexus of migrants through active citizenship

Website: https://nexus4civics.eu/

Runtime: September 2019 – August 2022

Supported / co-funded by: Erasmus+ Programme of the European Union

Partners: UNED – Universidad Nacional de Educacion a Distancia, Spain (coordinator); European Citizen Action Service, Belgium; Institute for the Development of Education, Croatia; Knowledge Innovation Centre, Malta; Malmo University, Sweden; UNIMED – Mediterranean University Union, Italy; Zavod Za Avtorsko Produkcijo Izobrazevanje Inovativnost in Sodelovanje, Slovenia.

Project representative to be contacted for further info: Beatriz Sedano Cuevas (bsedano@invi.uned.es)

Main target groups of the project: Higher Education students with a migrant background

Significant public results: The overarching goal of the project is to empower migrant students to explore the relationship between participatory digital tools and democracy, by innovating civic education at higher education institutions (HEIs).

The project is arranged around four pillars of activity:

- **Pillar 1: Civic education micro-learning units,** which will lead to the production of a MOOC on Civic education for students with migration background;
- **Pillar 2: Community engagement (learning) and service-learning guidelines for Universities**, through the creation of a knowledge-sharing platform for civics-educators, focused on migration, and guidelines for HEIs on student's civic engagement, focusing on the nexus family-community-civil society-state-HEI. A strategic framework on civic engagement of HEIs will emphasize how service-learning can address the needs of migrant students' inclusion;
- **Pillar 3: Re-wiring Civics to 4.0: connecting students to institutions in the digital age**, through the compilation of an inventory of digital tools for Open Democracy and digital citizenship education, a handbook for educators on civic education for a digital age and the organisation of a training seminar for educators on the same topic.

The expected impact of NEXUS is to enable and support HEIs in recognizing the value of different citizenship styles and emerging online environments that may supplement or supplant civic knowledge of diverse student bodies.

Human and Artificial Intelligence for the Society of the Future
Short Paper Book of the European Distance and E-Learning Network (EDEN)
2020 Annual Conference | Timisoara, 22-24 June, 2020
ISBN 978-615-5511-28-8

MODE-IT

Curricular modernization by implementing MOOCs model

Website: https://mode-it.eu/

Runtime: 10.2019 – 12.2021

Supported / co-funded by: Erasmus+ Strategic Partnerships for Higher Education

Partners: Fachhochschule des Mittelstands (Bielefeld/ Germany) (co-ordinator); Kaunas University of Technology (KTU) (Lithuania); Politehnica University of Timisoara (Romania); Anadolu University (Eskisehir/ Turkey); Instituto Politecnico do Porto (Portugal).

Project representative to be contacted for further info: Tim Brueggemann (brueggemann@fh-mittelstand.de), Diana Andone (diana.andone@upt.ro)

The buzzword MOOC causes in Europe both, praise and criticism. MOOCs provide to everybody a unique opportunity to enjoy higher education services for free, without having enrolled in a university, and have greater potentials to building up a digital knowledge-based society.

However, only about 5% of enrolled learners are able to complete a MOOC. Why? The fact is: learning via MOOCs requires additional transversal skills from learners, such as the ability of self-regulated learning, analytical and research skills, and advanced digital competence.

The vast MOOC attendees seem simply not prepared for open online learning formats due to missing competences needed to benefit from such type of studies.

The **MODE IT team** believes these competences should be acquired by learners already during their formal studies. The innovative MODE IT solution is: to integrate MOOC-based teaching and learning approaches into higher education curricula! Formal students should learn via MOOCs and increase in this manner not only their subject knowledge, but also train the ability of lifelong learning!

MODE IT stands for the Erasmus+ project „Curricular modernization by implementing MOOCs model". Five MODE IT partners from Germany, Lithuania, Turkey, Portugal, and Romania jointly seek to introduce innovative MOOC-based approaches to the design and delivery of higher education courses. In other words, open online formats will be integrated into formal education towards making it more flexible and attractive for students.

This innovative MODE IT approach should contribute to:

- Raising awareness of open learning formats by students for their future self-development;
- Taking responsibility of own learning by students;
- Increasing the ability to self-regulated and personalized learning.

The main innovation drivers of MODE IT approach are academic staff! Therefore, MODE IT specific objectives are:

- To create awareness of professional (self)-development amongst academic staff;
- To enhance skills of academic staff in the design and delivery of MOOCs and MOOC-based curricula;
- To create and deliver MOOC-based subjects within selected higher education curricula.

MODE-IT – Curricular modernization by implementing MOOCs model

Main target groups of the project: academic staff, students, higher education stakeholders

Significant public results: MODE IT expected outputs:

- Online self-assessment tool: to support academic staff when identifying their individual needs for the design and delivery of MOOC-based teaching and learning scenarios
- Open online training program for development and implementation of MOOC-based curricula
- MOOC-based higher education curricula to embedding MOOC into HEI curricula will be piloted at MODE IT institutions

Abstract

MODE IT is an Erasmus+ project "Curricular modernization by implementing MOOCs model" with partners from Germany, Lithuania, Turkey, Portugal, and Romania that, jointly, seek to introduce innovative MOOC-based approaches to the design and delivery of higher education courses. Open online formats will be integrated into formal education towards making it more flexible and attractive for students.